7 Strategies for Improving Your School

This book provides the busiest leaders with an accessible set of tools that can immediately be deployed to positively impact their school. Authors Ronald Williamson and Barbara R. Blackburn explore the COMPASS model—Culture; Ownership and Shared Vision; Managing Data; Professional Development; Advocacy; Shared Accountability; and Structures to Sustain Success—as an overall framework for school improvement. Chapters include in-depth discussions of easy-to-implement, useful strategies for improvement and address the most common concerns facing today's school leaders. Supplemented with templates, charts, and other adaptable tools for ongoing, practical use, *7 Strategies for Improving Your School* is your key guide to school improvement.

Ronald Williamson is Professor of Educational Leadership at Eastern Michigan University, USA. He is a former principal, central office administrator, and Executive Director of the National Middle School Association (now AMLE).

Barbara R. Blackburn, a "Top 30 Global Guru in Education," is a bestselling author and sought-after consultant. She was an award-winning professor at Winthrop University and has taught students of all ages. In addition to speaking at conferences worldwide, she also regularly presents workshops for teachers and administrators.

Other Eye on Education Books Available From Routledge
(www.routledge.com/eyeoneducation)

Rigor is NOT a Four-Letter Word, 3rd Edition
Barbara R. Blackburn

Advocacy from A to Z
Robert Blackburn, Barbara R. Blackburn, Ronald Williamson

Rigor in Your School: A Toolkit for Leaders, 2nd Edition
Ronald Williamson and Barbara R. Blackburn

The Principalship from A to Z, 2nd Edition
Ronald Williamson and Barbara R. Blackburn

Leading Schools in an Era of Declining Resources
J. Howard Johnston and Ronald Williamson

The School Leader's Guide to Social Media
Ronald Williamson and J. Howard Johnston

Get Organized! Time Management for School Leaders, 2nd Edition
Frank Buck

Rigor in Your Classroom: A Toolkit for Teachers
Barbara R. Blackburn

Motivating Struggling Learners: 10 Ways to Build Student Success
Barbara R. Blackburn

Leadership in America's Best Urban Schools
Joseph F. Johnson, Jr., Cynthia L. Uline, and Lynne G. Perez

The Educational Leader's Guide for School Scheduling: Strategies Addressing Grades K–12
Elliot Y. Merenbloom and Barbara A. Kalina

7 Strategies for Improving Your School

**Ronald Williamson and
Barbara R. Blackburn**

Routledge
Taylor & Francis Group
NEW YORK AND LONDON

First published 2020
by Routledge
52 Vanderbilt Avenue, New York, NY 10017

and by Routledge
2 Park Square, Milton Park, Abingdon, Oxon, OX14 4RN

Routledge is an imprint of the Taylor & Francis Group, an informa business

© 2020 Taylor & Francis

The right of Ronald Williamson and Barbara R. Blackburn to be identified as authors of this work has been asserted by them in accordance with sections 77 and 78 of the Copyright, Designs and Patents Act 1988.

All rights reserved. The purchase of this copyright material confers the right on the purchasing institution to photocopy or download pages which bear the eResources icon and a copyright line at the bottom of the page. No other parts of this book may be reprinted or reproduced or utilised in any form or by any electronic, mechanical, or other means, now known or hereafter invented, including photocopying and recording, or in any information storage or retrieval system, without permission in writing from the publishers.

Trademark notice: Product or corporate names may be trademarks or registered trademarks, and are used only for identification and explanation without intent to infringe.

Library of Congress Cataloging-in-Publication Data
Names: Williamson, Ronald D., author. | Blackburn, Barbara R., 1961– author.
Title: 7 strategies for improving your school / by Ronald Williamson and Barbara R. Blackburn.
Other titles: Seven strategies for improving your school
Description: New York : Routledge, 2019. | Includes bibliographical references.
Identifiers: LCCN 2019012265 | ISBN 9781138391451 (hardback) | ISBN 9781138391482 (pbk.) | ISBN 9780429422690 (ebook)
Subjects: LCSH: School improvement programs—United States.
Classification: LCC LB2822.82 .W559 2019 | DDC 371.2/07—dc23
LC record available at https://lccn.loc.gov/2019012265

ISBN: 978-1-138-39145-1 (hbk)
ISBN: 978-1-138-39148-2 (pbk)
ISBN: 978-0-429-42269-0 (ebk)

Typeset in Palatino
by Apex CoVantage LLC

Visit the eResources: www.routledge.com/9781138391482

I dedicate this book to my four grandchildren. You are a constant source of amazement and pride. I'm optimistic about the future because of your zeal for life, your competitiveness and drive, your compassion for those around you and for your passion to make the world a better place for everyone.
—*Ronald Williamson*

I dedicate this book to the Australian Council of Educational Leaders and those leaders I have met in Australia. You are committed to making a difference for your teachers and students, and I have tremendous respect for you.
—*Barbara R. Blackburn*

Contents

Meet the Authors ix
Introduction xi
Acknowledgments xiii
eResources xv

1. Overview and Introduction of the COMPASS Model for School Improvement   1
2. A Positive and Supportive Culture   11
3. Ownership and Shared Vision   25
4. Managing Data   39
5. Professional Development   59
6. Advocacy   79
7. Shared Accountability   99
8. Structures to Support School Improvement   115
9. Improving Your School: Making It Happen   131
10. Common Concerns   153

References   173

Meet the Authors

Ronald Williamson is a Professor of Educational Leadership at Eastern Michigan University. He is a former principal, central office administrator, and Executive Director of the National Middle School Association (now AMLE). Ron has authored more than 100 books, chapters, and articles in all of the major publications serving teachers and administrators. *Phi Delta Kappa* recognized two of his publications as among the most essential readings in middle grades education. Ron is the recipient of the Gruhn-Long-Melton Award from NASSP in recognition of lifetime achievement in middle grades leadership. His most recent books include *Rigor in Your School: A Toolkit for Leaders* and *The Principalship from A to Z*. Ron can be reached through his website http://ronwilliamson.com.

Barbara R. Blackburn, named a Top 30 Global Guru in Education, has dedicated her life to raising the level of rigor and motivation for professional educators and students alike. What differentiates Barbara's over 20 books are her easily executable concrete examples based on decades of experience as a teacher, professor, and consultant. Barbara's dedication to education was inspired in her early years by her parents. Her father's doctorate and lifetime career as a professor taught her the importance of professional training. Her mother's career as school secretary shaped Barbara's appreciation of the effort all staff play in the education of every student. Barbara has taught early childhood, elementary, middle, and high school students and has served as an educational consultant for three publishing companies. She holds a master's degree in school administration and was certified as a teacher and school principal in North Carolina. She received her Ph.D. in Curriculum and Teaching from the University of North Carolina at Greensboro. In 2006, she received the award for Outstanding Junior Professor at Winthrop University. She left her position at the University of North Carolina at Charlotte to write and speak full time.

In addition to speaking at state, national, and international conferences, she also regularly presents workshops for teachers and administrators in elementary, middle, and high schools. Her workshops are lively and engaging and filled with practical information. Her most popular topics include:

- Rigor is NOT a Four-Letter Word;
- Rigorous Schools and Classrooms: Leading the Way;

- Rigorous Assessments;
- Differentiating Instruction Without Lessening Rigor in Your Classroom;
- Motivation + Engagement + Rigor = Student Success;
- Rigor for Students With Special Needs;
- Motivating Struggling Students.

Barbara can be reached through her website: www.barbarablackburnonline.com.

Introduction

If you've picked up this book, you are probably looking for ways to improve your school. Despite the number of books, articles, and workshops on this topic, we wanted to approach the issue in a new way, one that would be particularly practical for school leaders.

In Chapter 1, we'll provide an overview, or roadmap to the book. First, we use the notion of a compass to describe seven strategies that can help you. The COMPASS stands for Culture, Ownership and Shared Vision, Managing Data, Professional Development, Advocacy, Shared Accountability, and Structures to Sustain Success. Chapter 9 will provide a base for your COMPASS, addressing a model of change. The focus throughout each chapter is on easy-to-implement, useful strategies you can use immediately, and on an ongoing basis.

Chapter 10 builds on the practical concepts and addresses the common concerns we hear most often from leaders. These include motivating your teachers, recruiting teachers, responding to overly negative teachers, dealing with limited resources, and balancing work with the rest of your life. If you are feeling particularly overwhelmed with any of these issues, consider starting with Chapter 10.

Throughout the chapters you'll find templates, charts, and other tools you can use. Many of these are also available online at www.routledge.com/9781138391482. You'll also find Collaboration Connections, which provide ideas to collaborate with students, business partners, and other stakeholders. To close each chapter, you will see a Where Do I Begin two-column chart, which details different issues, such as *If you want to assess your current efforts,* **Then** *start with the advocacy pre-assessment*. The if-then approach will allow you to prioritize the tools.

Finally, consider this book as a guide to school improvement. There will be times you want to adapt a tool or strategy, and other times there will be one that doesn't fit your situation. That is fine. We've provided a wide variety of tools so that you can choose the one that best suits your needs. We hope the tools and strategies help you navigate your journey to school improvement. If you'd like to reach us, contact Ron at ronwilliamson.com and Barbara at www.barbarablackburnonline.com.

Acknowledgments

- Ron's colleagues in the Department of Leadership and Counseling at Eastern Michigan University.
- Barbara's network of support for her work, which includes her husband, Pete; her stepson, Hunter; her parents; extended family members; and Abbigail Armstrong.
- John Maloney for a fabulous cover design.
- Autumn Spalding of Apex CoVantage for production and design.
- Heather Jarrow for her ongoing support as our editor.
- Thank you to the hundreds of school leaders we've worked with in every part of the nation. Leadership is a demanding job. We respect your work and your commitment to a quality educational experience for every student. We value our time together and the opportunity to learn from you. Your work and your ideas made this book a practical guide for school leaders.

eResources

Resources mentioned in this book can be downloaded, printed, used to copy/paste text, and/or manipulated to suit your individualized use. You can access these downloads by visiting the book product page on our website www.routledge.com/9781138391482. Then click on the tab that reads "eResources" and then select the file(s) you need. The file(s) will download directly to your computer.

Tool	Page Number
Impacting School Culture: Positive and Negative	13
Leadership Self-Assessment	22
Process for Developing a School Vision Statement	33
Data Crosswalk	52
Assess Your Professional Development Efforts	61
Professional Learning Communities: Assess Your Own Dispositions	65
Reflective Guide	70
Self-Assess Your Advocacy Skills	80
Working With Internal Stakeholders	83
Parent and Family Advocacy Tools	90
Advocacy Scorecard	96
Checklist of Planning Activities	139

1

Overview and Introduction of the COMPASS Model for School Improvement

Whether you're a principal, curriculum coordinator, superintendent, or teacher leader, you've likely faced the challenge of school improvement. Improving a school, including student learning, is a complex task. It often feels like it's difficult to stay on top of the issues let alone deal with the competing interests and priorities from every stakeholder group.

Over the past 35 years we've worked in hundreds of schools in every region of the country and served every type of school community. We've watched the struggle. We've applauded the successes and we've supported those whose initiatives didn't achieve the results they envisioned.

Those experiences inform this book and the model we suggest for school improvement. We believe that change is not an event but rather a journey. We recognize that schools are in a constant state of change. They are shaped by demographic, social, political, and economic factors of contemporary American society. Because of those factors, schools change a little each day in response to state and national issues, parent and community demands, and new research and knowledge about student learning.

The most successful schools are those that recognize that change is a constant, that improvement is a journey, not an event. Just like a road, the process has multiple paths and you may suddenly approach an intersection and find yourself needing to change routes. You might find yourself looping back, covering the same stretch of road more than once, or making unplanned stops along the way. You may even encounter potholes or bumps in the road.

The journey to becoming a more successful school is not straight, but often winding. To successfully navigate that road it is important to have a good set of tools—a roadmap, useful contact information, and a GPS unit or compass.

The COMPASS Model

A few years ago, following a presentation, we were talking about the many approaches to school improvement. We talked about the questions from participants and that led to a much longer conversation about the complexities of school improvement.

That conversation led to talk about how we conceptualized school improvement. We both find a compass to be a good metaphor to understand the way leaders can positively impact their school. A compass provides direction and guidance. It can help you find your way when lost and help you stay on track. Most importantly, a compass stays on "true" north and constantly remains on target.

After those initial conversations we shared our thinking with teachers and principals in schools across the country. We asked about their experience with school improvement. We listened as they described their successes and their challenges. We took notes on strategies and tools they found useful. And we used their practical, on-the-ground experience with school improvement to inform our model.

We created the COMPASS model as a way to capture both the complexity of school improvement and to demonstrate the connections between each of the components. Here's a brief overview of the seven strategies for improving your school.

C—Creating a Positive and Supportive Culture

We've discovered that to make significant change in a school's program a leader must understand the school's culture and incorporate strategies that will allow them to positively impact the culture.

When we talk about culture, we are talking about the complex set of values, traditions, and patterns of behavior present in a school. A school's culture reflects deeply held beliefs about students and schooling. It manifests itself in "the unwritten rules and assumptions, the combination of rituals and traditions, the array of symbols and artifacts, the special language and phrasing that staff and students use, the expectations for change and learning" (Deal & Peterson, 2016).

Principals recognize the importance of cultural symbols. They use these symbols to promote the institutional values and the school's core mission. Successful principals understand the power of these cultural symbols to telegraph what is important.

Successful principals model the behaviors and practices that they expect others to use. It is important to use constructive language, support risk-taking, and build relationships.

Chapter 2 will discuss the importance of culture in more depth and provide strategies and tools that leaders can use to assure a culture supportive of the success of every student.

O—Ownership and Shared Vision

When all the critical stakeholders are engaged in the process, their collective commitment to change is greater (David, 2009; Hord, 2009). Research also shows that when teachers and others collaborate on instructional issues, their practice is more likely to change (Borko, 2004).

When we work with teachers, families, and other school personnel, we almost always find that they have very different ideas about school improvement and how it should shape their schools. These different ideas mean that it is important to involve each group in any discussion about refining and strengthening your school.

If your school's mission statement has not been updated in several years, it may be appropriate to review it and make needed changes. Schools change in subtle ways over time. Students are different, the community changes, the economic and social issues change. All of these can lead to changes in a school's mission.

Ownership and shared vision are one of the essential components of our COMPASS model and will be discussed in Chapter 3.

M—Managing Data

Groups that use members' opinions as the primary source of data almost always become contentious. We've found that the most constructive groups are characterized by the gathering and analysis of data independent of any individual's experience or opinion.

It is essential to gather data about student learning. Put together a portfolio of materials that reflect the academic expectations of students, the quality of their work, and agreed-upon measures of academic success.

It may also be useful to conduct a self-assessment of your school's program. A brief survey or other instrument can be used to gather data from teachers, parents, students, and others about the state of the instructional program. One principal we knew used a simple rubric to assess classroom practices. At a staff meeting, groups of teachers worked together to complete the rubric. These data were then used by the School Improvement Team to guide the discussion about their program.

Another way to provide data may be to gather data directly from students. Ron helped a school in Connecticut design an assessment to be completed by students. First, the faculty agreed on their indicators for an engaging academic program, then a short survey using a Likert scale was constructed. Individual students completed the survey and the results were aggregated by category (grade, gender) to provide information about how students perceived the engagement of their academic program.

These and other strategies will be discussed in Chapter 4.

P—Professional Development

Also essential to improving your school's program is providing teachers and other staff with appropriate professional development. The principal can set the direction for a school's professional development agenda. It is important that the principal model a commitment to continuous improvement and be an active participant in professional development activities.

We've found that the most successful professional development is focused on increasing the capacity of the staff. Too often professional development consists of workshops, institutes, or seminars. The most successful models include a wider variety of activities such as collaborative work teams, study groups, critical friends groups, peer coaching, and external support, such as partnerships and networks focused on specific knowledge and skills.

Learning Forward (2019) recommends that professional development focuses on improving the learning of all students by organizing adults into learning groups or communities whose goals are aligned with those of the school or district. The groups use disaggregated student data to determine adult learning priorities and sustain improvement, and deepen educators' content knowledge and instructional capacity.

At Tucson High School, Principal Abel Morado organized his staff into a set of small learning communities. Each group, either content or interdisciplinary, selected a goal related to the school's mission and identified data they would collect about their progress. During monthly meetings the work groups reviewed their data, discussed their progress, and identified steps for continued progress. Dr. Morado described the process,

> At first they were reluctant. We'd never done anything like this before. So we focused on developing the skills to work together. There's room for improvement, but it is going well. Teachers are talking with one another about students and their learning.

Chapter 5 will explore the importance of professional development in more depth.

A—Advocacy

What leaders pay attention to becomes important (Schein, 2016), and it is important that school leaders express support for and advocate for their school's improvement efforts. Advocacy is a way to press for changes in your school. It is also a way to build support for your school's vision and to secure resources to support that vision.

School leaders must advocate with many diverse audiences, both internal and external. They must work with teachers and other staff to assure a shared commitment to school improvement. They must work with families and community to understand the need for change and to cultivate their support. They must also work with district-level staff to make sure that their school has the flexibility and resources to support the school's vision.

One important first step is to build a network with others who share your vision. But don't limit your contact with just those who share your point of view. Talk with those who hold other opinions. Monitor your environment. Get to know the "movers and shakers" in your community. Finally, identify your allies and your opponents so that you can build alliances in support of your vision.

Successful advocacy is more than just having a passion for your vision to improve your school. It requires developing a thoughtful and compelling message about the importance of what you propose and identifying strategies to share your vision and mobilize support.

Chapter 6 will provide you with a set of useful tools that you can use to design your advocacy plan and to build support for your vision.

S—Shared Accountability

We believe that one of the biggest roadblocks to school improvement is the resistance from teachers, parents, and others. As we discussed earlier, every person deals differently with change. Some are more accepting; others more resistant.

No change is successful unless accountability is established. We suggest that teachers, families, and community, along with school leaders, are accountable for improving your school.

Accountability is more than issuing mandates and forcing compliance. For school leaders it involves energizing and motivating individuals as well as groups.

As we discussed earlier, the culture of the school must be one where high value is placed on improving students' educational experience, where there is a collective commitment to improvement, and a parallel commitment to supporting people who take risks and make changes. Further, the culture must not accept failure as an option. Every student must be expected to learn and the staff must be committed to supporting students in their learning.

The most important role of a school leader is instructional leader. But the principal is not the only person responsible for a quality instructional program. Teachers and other staff are responsible for delivering instruction and positively impacting every student's learning.

School leaders, however, are responsible for creating a climate and culture at their school that supports quality instruction, promotes innovation, and nurtures professional growth. You can do this by:

- Providing time for collegial discussion and dialogue about improved instruction, including time to reflect on efforts to improve the education of every student;
- Staying current on educational trends and developments;
- Modeling quality instructional practices at meetings and during other interaction with staff; and
- Attending and actively participating in professional development and other learning opportunities.

Shared accountability is critical to efforts to improve schools. Chapter 7 will discuss the issue in more depth and provide additional ideas that you can use in your school to build a collective commitment to the success of every student.

S—Structures

The day-to-day routines and structures of your school can impact your ability to improve your school. Structures, frequently rooted in past practice, can be major barriers to reform or they can be used to accelerate achieving your vision.

In many schools the most significant structural barrier is the isolation of teachers from one another. Many schools have created professional learning communities (PLCs). While PLCs take many forms, they almost always focus on student learning and value time for teachers and administrators to work together to talk about student learning and decide how to improve their school.

The design of the school's schedule is another important structural factor. Designing a schedule to provide collaborative time, to organize teachers into collaborative instructional groups, and to provide students with opportunities to receive extra support are essential.

School policies and practices, such as homework and grading procedures, are also structures that can promote or inhibit school change.

Structures that can support your school improvement efforts will be examined in Chapter 8. It is the final element of our COMPASS model.

Before You Begin

People respond to change in many different ways. That is especially true when the conversation deals with change in schools.

We once heard a speaker compare the impact of change to crossing a busy street on a foggy day. Before any change, people are on the cement curb on one side of the street. They know that once they get to the other side they will once again be standing on a solid cement curb. The difficulty is that people must step away from the safety of the curb they know, walk into a foggy street, and be confident that they will successfully get to the other side.

The leader's role is to help people navigate foggy streets, to provide the confidence that the future will be secure, and to assure that people will be supported throughout the change.

Check Your Own Assumptions

We all hold assumptions about things. Those assumptions are based on our experiences and reflect our own unique, idiosyncratic experiences. In any group, its members bring to the conversation a whole set of very different assumptions.

> **What Assumptions Do You Hold?**
> - What do you believe about change?
> - What motivation strategies work most successfully with your school community?
> - How quickly do you believe your school can change?
> - What conditions are most likely to result in a more effective school?
> - Is your vision for change the one that should be implemented?

Most organizations, including schools, resist change. You've probably heard many of these before. They are often used to justify keeping things the way they are. "Let sleeping dogs lie." "If it ain't broke, don't fix it." "Just wait a couple of years and this principal (superintendent) will be gone." "We tried it once before and it didn't work."

Schools are expected to assume greater responsibility for helping students adapt, and indeed thrive, in a changing world. This means you need to examine the very essence of your school, your core beliefs, and how they impact teaching and learning.

Over the years we've learned a lot about how schools change. We've learned that key stakeholders must be involved. We know that it almost always involves conflict and disagreement, and that real change takes time and sustained effort.

> **The Leader and Change**
> - Effective change takes time. It is a process of development and requires persistence.
> - The complexity of change means that everyone may not agree on what is proposed.
> - Conflict and disagreement are part of the process and help to clarify beliefs and next steps. They are fundamental to successful change.
> - Any significant change requires those implementing the change to be involved and make their own meaning.
> - The lack of implementation may not be rejection of the change. It may be lack of time or other resources.
> - Change is really about changing the culture of your school.
> - People respond best when conditions allow them to react to ideas, form their own position, interact with others, and be provided with professional development and other technical assistance.
>
> *Source:* Adapted from Fullan (2001, 2015); Glickman, Gordon, & Ross-Gordon (2018)

Use Positive and Supportive Leadership Behaviors

Successful leaders model the behaviors and practices that they expect others to use. It is important to use constructive language, support risk-taking, and build relationships.

We've found that when principals talk with teachers and other staff about instructional issues, it is valuable to use language and practices that open the communication rather than close it. In particular, we've found the following characterize constructive group dynamics:

- Listen, don't get defensive;
- Ask questions, don't accuse;
- Respect the complexity of change; don't expect immediate results;
- Value different points of view; don't tell people what to believe;
- Value collaboration; don't expect agreement on everything;
- Trust people to do the right thing; don't demand compliance.

It is important that leaders be active and engaged learners, that they demonstrate their support for any instructional change.

Final Thoughts

Most changes in schools take place in response to events (different students, societal trends). These events help to identify a need. Schools respond to these emerging needs in one of three ways—ignore them, reject them, or address them.

A starkly different approach is a much more thoughtful and deliberative planning process. We suggest that when you work with your community to improve your school, it is best to use a deliberative process, one that involves important stakeholders, provides for discussion about approaches and strategies, utilizes a collaborative approach to making decisions, regularly collects data about progress, and develops the capacity to sustain the work.

Before you move any further in *7 Strategies for Improving Your School*, we'd like to ask you to stop and think about your vision for your school. If your school, classroom, or district were truly committed to improving the educational experience of every student, what would that look like? How would your teachers and students be different? What would you be doing differently than you are today? Take a few moments, sit down with a blank sheet of paper, and sketch out your vision—either in narrative, bullet points, or diagrams. Then hold onto it, we'll come back to this towards the end of the book.

2

A Positive and Supportive Culture

Culture reflects the complex set of values, traditions, and patterns of behavior that are present in a school. Unlike school climate, a school's culture is indicative of the deeply embedded beliefs about schooling and reveals itself in "the unwritten rules and assumptions, the combination of rituals and traditions, the array of symbols and artifacts, the special language and phrasing that staff and students use, the expectations for change and learning" (Peterson & Deal, 2002, p. 9). A school's culture is reflected in the things that occur every day at the school. Often those behaviors have become so routine that they are just accepted as "the way we do things around here" and that is the street-level definition of culture.

It is those patterns of behavior and those unwritten, and often unspoken, assumptions about students, families, and student learning that shape a culture. For example, there is often a tension between the importance of athletics and academics. If a community chose to spend more on an athletic facility than on school renovations, it says something about values. Or if a school adopted a stance that every child will read by the end of the second grade, it says something about values.

> **Sample Assumptions**
> - All students can learn at very high levels;
> - Middle school students are active and fidgety;
> - Some families don't care a lot about education;
> - This community always supports schools.

The culture of a school is a powerful tool that leaders can use to shape the operation of their school and the behavior of those who work there (Williamson & Johnston, 2005). As schools face pressure to change, the introduction of reforms introduces uncertainty and unpredictability into the lives of people working in schools. Because culture is central to any organization, including schools, understanding how it works and how it can be shaped is an important tool for improving a school's educational program.

The concept of school culture emerged from the work of Deal and Kennedy (1982), Deal and Peterson (2016), and Schein (2016). Two key ideas are central to the concept. First, a school's culture reflects the informal, often unspoken, rules about how people behave. Second, a positive school culture can "enable people to feel better about what they do" (Deal & Kennedy, 1982, p. 16).

Role of the Leader

Successful school leaders are skilled at diagnosing and monitoring their school's culture, assessing what works to support the school's vision and mission, and modifying those patterns of behavior to support their school's vision of an effective and engaging academic experience for students.

During one school visit we spoke with a new principal who commented, "The culture in this school is just very traditional. I'm the new person, and there's really nothing I can do to change it." We disagree. Of course, it will take time, focus, and patience, but a leader can change the culture of their school. Another principal we worked with stated it well, "The school leader is most influential in creating and maintaining a positive culture. Without leadership, expectations will wane and outcomes will be mixed at best."

Schein (2016) identified a set of tools that leaders can use to embed and reinforce new cultural norms in their organization. They include the leader's response to critical events; their modeling, teaching, and coaching of other personnel; the criteria used to reward and recognize staff; and most importantly, what the leader pays attention to and measures.

> **Ways Leaders Can Impact Their School's Culture**
>
> - What leaders pay attention to, measure, and control becomes important;
> - The leader's reactions to critical incidents and events;
> - Role modeling, teaching, and coaching by leaders;
> - The criteria for allocation of rewards and status in the school; and
> - Criteria used for recruitment, selection, and promotion.
>
> *Source:* Adapted from Schein (2016)

Let's look at practical examples that can positively or negatively influence your school's culture.

Impacting School Culture: Positive and Negative

Do This	Not That
Laser focusing on most important tasks, authentic data collection related to area of improvement.	Placing a focus on minutia or things you cannot control.
Reacting with a sense of calm, assuring others you are in control/have a plan.	Reacting with a sense of panic, showing and expressing negative emotions.
When appropriate, leaders offer to teach in classrooms. They model a commitment to student learning and the school's vision through words and actions. Coaching is positive and focused on progress, not evaluation.	Rarely visiting classrooms unless required and feedback on evaluations reflects a lack of understanding of instruction. Modeling does not reflect the vision of the school, and words and actions may actually negate the vision. Coaching is non-existent or negative.
Promotions to teacher leadership or other leadership positions as well as receipt of recognition is based on quality, and commitment to student learning and the school's vision, not seniority.	Rewards and promotions are awarded based on tenure and seniority, with no consideration of quality and commitment to the vision.

Do This	Not That
Leaders clearly explain the vision of the school during recruiting efforts, hire faculty who are committed to the same vision, and teachers are offered promotions to teacher leadership and other leadership positions based on their ongoing actions toward positive change.	Leaders are focused on finding and hiring teachers to fill their teaching shortage, so vision becomes secondary. Promoting faculty is determined by ensuring that teachers do not leave.

Assessing Your Culture

Successful school leaders recognize the power of culture to shape their school. They develop the capacity to deploy the tools in ways that reinforce the importance of the vision for their school's program. You might want to make a quick assessment of your school's culture. If so, here are some things you might do to assess the culture of your school.

Ways to Assess Culture

- At a staff meeting, ask each person to list five adjectives that describe the school's culture. Organize the words into common themes. Discuss their meaning.
- Walk the halls of your school. What do you see? What artifacts are visible that convey messages about student success? About the value of rigorous work? About a commitment to not accepting failure?
- Talk with a cross-section of teachers or students. What gets them excited about their work? About their learning? What do they find joy in?
- Consider the last three months. What have you done to show your enthusiasm for learning? For student success? How have you recognized and rewarded students and staff?

After you gather some of these data, identify any patterns you may find. What do they say about the culture in your school? How might you use the symbols of culture to improve your school?

Aspects of School Culture

Bolman and Deal (2017) developed a model for understanding the things that contribute to culture. It is based on the idea that every organization has a culture that reflects underlying values, and patterns of shared basic assumptions. These assumptions are often taught to new members of the culture, whether teachers, students, or parents, as the "way we do things around here" (Bower, 1996).

Over time every school develops its own personality. This is shaped by the people who work in the school, the community the school serves, the students who attend the school and the way these groups respond to the successes, tragedies, and daily events at the school. Culture is a powerful set of rituals, traditions, and practices that reflect the values of a school.

When a leader understands these elements of culture and how they reflect a school community's values and beliefs, they can use them to promote institutional values and the school's core mission. Most importantly, if you understand the power of these symbols, you can use them to telegraph messages about "what is important."

Element	Description	Examples
Rituals and Ceremonies	They provide structure to our daily life and to the routine of a school. Rituals occur rather routinely while ceremonies are grander, less frequent events (graduation). Both rituals and ceremonies reflect values in their structure, their priority, and carry meaning about what is valued and what is important.	Focus of school assemblies and other ceremonies Daily announcements or daily bulletins
Heroes and Heroines	Those people who are looked up to as reflecting the organization's values; people who are examples of living the values.	Informal teacher leaders Teachers admired by others for their work with students
Stories and Tales	Those recollections of events that are told and retold and play a powerful role in sharing examples of organizational values. Stories often contain a moral and are inevitably engaging.	Stories shared with parents and other members of the school community Examples told to new teachers

Element	Description	Examples
Rewards and Reinforcements	They reflect those things that are valued and therefore rewarded. Is it creativity in the classroom or compliance with established patterns? Is it waiving a rule so that a student may be successful or adhering to established policy?	Formal and informal recognition systems Use of budget for instructional materials and professional development

Source: Adapted from Bolman and Deal (2017), Deal and Peterson (2016)

Rituals and Ceremonies

Every day teachers, students, and administrators participate in routines that are just accepted as the way things should be done. They begin when students arrive at school, how they move from classroom to classroom, how attendance is taken, or how lunch is managed. Those routines are often not thought of as a reflection of culture but each one, and the hundreds of other routines, are based on assumptions about students, student behavior, and the need to manage the school day.

Similarly, schools occasionally have special activities and events like field trips, assemblies, or pep rallies. The type of event, and the content of those events, also reflects underlying values about what is important.

Understanding how those rituals and ceremonies reflect a school's culture allows a leader to develop a plan to use those activities to support and nurture the values and beliefs in the school's core mission. For example, in addition to celebrating top grades, a school can celebrate progress toward higher levels of achievement. In addition to an honor roll, publish a "Principal's Progress" list, which recognizes any student who has made progress over a certain period of time.

Principal's Progress Sample Items

- Students who increased grades or grade point averages;
- Students who moved from a "not yet" to a minimum grade;
- Students who revised work during an extra help session;
- Students who support the academic progress of other students.

One Michigan middle school starts every year with an opening day celebration. Students march to the athletic field carrying banners with their team name. Students who made exceptional academic progress the prior year are recognized and incoming students are introduced to the school's motto—"Excellence, Excellence, Excellence." Following the ceremony every team meets to set academic goals for the year and to talk about how exceptional student performance will be recognized.

A high school in Oregon begins the school year with a special welcoming for incoming ninth graders. Teachers, staff, and tenth, eleventh, and twelfth grade students line the hallways and greet the incoming students. Every ninth grader is recognized and provided a student mentor. Similarly, at the end of the year, the senior class is recognized on their final day of school. Teachers, staff, and ninth, tenth, and eleventh grade students line the hallways and applaud as the seniors depart.

Those are examples of two ceremonies that transmit important messages about what is valued and what is important.

Assess Your School...

- What regular routines tell you about the instructional program in your school?
- Is there a set of routines and rituals that clearly communicate your values about school and schooling? Do they work?
- Are there special ceremonies or events at your school that demonstrate a commitment to the success of every student?
- Do you use the recruitment and hiring of new teachers as a way to communicate values and shape culture?

A principal in Connecticut talked with Ron about how she makes sure that the hiring of new teachers conveys the school's commitment to a quality academic experience for every student.

> I've developed a set of questions that I ask of every candidate. If they're listening carefully, they will understand that this school values the success of every student and expects every student to succeed in an engaging and challenging environment.

The response from candidates provides this principal with clues about whether the candidates share the vision.

Heroes and Heroines

Who are the heroes and heroines in your effort to improve your school? Which teacher is considered the most supportive, but is also the most respected?

At Mill Creek Middle School, an old rowboat found when the school was constructed hangs in the office. An oar found with the boat has become an important way to recognize staff members for their exceptional commitment to the success of students. Principal Evelyn Shirk started the process to "encourage the staff to never, ever accept less than student success."

Every month the oar is given to one teacher who "goes over and above" in their work with students. The principal dresses up as an old boatsman and interrupts one of the classes of the person being recognized. After a brief ceremony the oar remains in the teacher's classroom as a very visible recognition of their commitment to student success.

Assess Your School. . .

- Who are the heroes or heroines on your staff? Why are they recognized?
- What ways do you identify and celebrate people who contribute to the success of every student? Who have high expectations for student success?
- Do you encourage the recognition of students and staff who positively contribute to the success of students?

In suburban Seattle an elementary school principal uses every opportunity to celebrate teachers who take risks that contribute to student success. A bulletin board near the school lobby was used to recognize "Explorer's Heroes." It included a picture and description of teachers, staff, or students who reflected the school's academic mission and commitment to "students will not fail."

As with any recognition program it was important to only recognize people who had made authentic contributions. For example, one teacher changed how she grouped students for instruction even when other teachers at her grade level resisted the change.

Collaboration Connection

Ask students and parents to help you recognize and reward teachers. Provide a simple reward certificate such as "Superstar Teacher," "You Make a Difference," or "You Matter to Me/My Son or Daughter."

Stories and Tales

Another indicator of culture has to do with the stories and tales about your school. They are much like an oral history, transmitted from family to family or from teacher to teacher.

What are the important stories that are told to newcomers? Are they stories about the support teachers feel when they promote standards from their students? Are new students told that their learning is not optional, that everyone in the school believes it is his or her responsibility to help each student learn? Do you hear turnaround stories about students who have overcome difficulties to learn at high levels?

The principal of a school in suburban Denver encouraged his teachers to "snitch" on other teachers who had some special success with students. Her goal was to find teachers who represented her school's commitment to a rigorous academic program complemented by high support. The principal delighted in sharing these stories with parents, with other district personnel, and with school staff. The goal was to create a culture of success and celebration of that success.

Similarly, a high school principal in suburban Tucson talked with Ron about how she worked with her staff to redesign the advisory program. Working with the School Improvement Team, they decided to provide increased academic support for students during this daily activity. The principal created a support and testing center where students could retake tests that they previously failed. One veteran teacher took the lead on the project and used her personal credibility to advocate for this "new" approach. The principal revels in telling the story of this teacher and how she put "her personal reputation on the line to make a difference in the lives of our students." It is a powerful story.

Assess Your School...

- How do you communicate verbally and through your actions your commitment to the success of every student? To increasing the success of your school's programs?
- What are the stories you tell about your school, its students, and staff? What stories do you encourage others to tell?
- What messages do you communicate in your daily actions, classroom visits, and other interactions with members of your school community?
- How do you nurture the storytellers on your staff? Do their stories reflect your school's values and mission?

It's also important to talk with your staff about the stories they tell. What do they say when talking with parents or community members? What examples do they provide about the school, its students, and its success?

The stories people tell and their recollection of events play a powerful role in shaping your school's culture. Successful school leaders recognize the power of words to shape culture. Our thoughts drive our feelings and our actions.

In *The Principalship from A to Z (2nd ed.)* (2016) we suggested a focus on the positive, the progress you make every day. We called that a "mental adjustment" and we encourage leaders to work with their teaches to "make a mental adjustment" in how they think about their school, and how they talk about their school.

Here are some examples of mental adjustments that we've seen schools make. Add to the list with examples from your own school.

Examples of Mental Adjustments

From Negative Thoughts	To Positive Thoughts
Why aren't our parents more involved?	What can we do to make our parents feel welcome?
Why doesn't our community value what we do?	How can we show the community we value them?
Why won't my students do their homework?	How can I include interesting and engaging activities in my lessons?
How can I get my students to learn this content?	How can we present the material so that it facilitates deep learning?
Why don't our students care about school?	What can we do to help our students become more interested in school?
Why isn't it possible to keep people happy?	What can I do today to have a positive interaction with everyone I meet?
How am I going to get everything done?	What am I going to do today that will make progress on my "to do" list?
Why can't all of our students meet standards?	How will I make a positive impact on one student today?

Reward System

The things that are recognized and rewarded also telegraph messages about what is valued and important. It's the final element of culture. What is the reward system—both formal and informal—in your school? Are teachers rewarded for working to address the needs of every student or are they rewarded for content completion? Are students rewarded for progress or just high schools? In one school we worked with, each teacher had a bulletin board called "Soaring to Success." Students chose what would be posted, following a simple criterion: "Where are you making progress and what are you proud of?" Postings ranged from drafts of writing to a reworking of a complicated math problem.

One way to promote recognition is "Name it, claim it, and explain it." As you see an example of quality instruction in a classroom, take a digital picture of what is happening. Begin each of your faculty meetings with a PowerPoint slide of what you saw. The first item on your agenda is always a celebration of something positive related to instruction. Ask your faculty, "I saw a great instructional strategy this week. It's up here on the screen. If it belongs to you, stand up and name what you did, claim it as yours, and explain what you were doing."

Regularly recognizing and celebrating positive examples of quality instruction will reinforce the commitment to schools and classrooms focused on the learning of every student.

Besides recognizing quality instruction, there are other things a principal does that sends messages about what is valued. Think about how you allocate funds for conference attendance or professional development. Is it equally distributed or is it distributed in support of school improvement goals? How do you use your school's budget? What gets recognized at end-of-the-year activities? What is displayed in your lobby or in your school's display cases?

Assess Your School...

- How do you recognize and reward teachers who reflect your school's commitment to quality learning? Are these strategies successful?
- Do you routinely reward teachers, staff, and students who make exceptional efforts to improve student learning?
- Do you allocate school resources, such as materials and professional development, in a way that rewards commitment to the school's vision and expectations?

We've also developed a *Leadership Self-Assessment* that you can use to examine how you currently use the elements of culture in your work.

Leadership Self-Assessment

	Guiding Questions	Examples From Your School
Rituals and Ceremonies	• What are the routines and rituals in your school? What values do they represent? • Are there special ceremonies or events at your school? What do they celebrate? • What messages do you communicate in your daily actions, classroom visits, and other interactions with members of your school community?	
Heroes and Heroines	• Who are the heroes or heroines on your staff? Why are they recognized? • What ways do you identify and celebrate people who contribute to the success of every student? Who has high expectations for student success?	
Stories and Tales	• How do you communicate verbally and through your actions with your faculty and staff? What underlying messages are represented? • What are the stories you tell about your school, its students, and staff? What stories do you encourage others to tell?	
Rewards and Reinforcements	• How do you recognize and reward teachers? What values are recognized and rewarded? Are these strategies successful? • Do you routinely reward teachers, staff, and students who make exceptional efforts to improve student learning?	

Structures to Support a Positive and Supportive Culture

Another way to impact the culture of a school is through structural elements. Without organizational structures to support change, it is like building castles in the air . . . you still need a ladder to get there.

There are organizational structures, or strategies, that can support your culture. Their absence can often inhibit development of a positive culture. We'll be discussing each of these in detail in upcoming chapters.

Structures

> Regular Data Analysis Meetings
> Identified Time for Collaboration
> Job-Embedded Professional Development
> Communication strategies using multiple media
> Schedules that support the shared vision

Leadership in Action: Shifting the Culture

In Tucson, Arizona Pueblo High School serves a largely Hispanic population of 1900 students. It has a large English as a Secondary Language population and is situated in a high-poverty neighborhood. When Pat Dienz became principal she found a school that needed rejuvenation. She described the school this way, "We needed to find a way to serve all of our students, to focus on student success, and to change the way we did things."

One thing that changed immediately was the way the principal talked about students and staff. Pat recognized the power of the stories she told to shape the culture of her school. She began to recognize teachers who "went over and above to help students." She also identified a core of teachers who shared her vision and were willing to work with her to change many of Pueblo's routines.

Of particular concern was the acceptance of student failure, and the unwillingness to change instructional practices. Pat began by focusing on improved instruction. She provided professional development for interested teachers and began a process to eliminate D's and E's, focusing on mastery with a revise-and-resubmit policy and creating a testing center where students could retake tests. She also launched an initiative to use the school's advisory program as a tool to promote student success. The program name changed to A.C.I. for Academic Check-In. This simple modification sent a powerful signal that advisory had a different focus.

A.C.I. groups consist of 20–25 students who work with one of their teachers. The time is used for Sustained Silent Reading and other forms of academic support. A testing center was created where students can go to take tests missed when absent or retake tests on which they were not successful. Students are also encouraged to "travel" to work with other teachers for tutoring or to make up missed work.

These changes didn't come about easily. In addition to telling stories about teacher leaders, Pat also began to recognize and talk about students who made significant changes in their academic success. More importantly, she persevered, recognizing that change does not occur quickly.

This principal recognized the power of stories, symbols, and routines to shape the way her school operated. She used the elements of culture to change the use of time and the commitment to student success.

Final Thoughts

As we said earlier, the culture of a school is a powerful tool for shaping the behavior of those who work and attend the school. It is important that principals recognize the way they can use the elements of culture to improve their school's commitment to every student.

Where Do I Begin?

If...	Then...
You want to see where you are now,	Start with the culture assessment.
You want specific strategies to shape culture,	Start with Bolman and Deal's Framework.
You want to help your teachers shift to a more positive attitude,	Share the mental adjustments with your teachers.
You need to organize our cultural elements to support our initiatives,	Start with the structures section.

3

Ownership and Shared Vision

Any initiative to improve your school requires the involvement of families and community as well as teachers and other school staff. Thus, it is important to involve all stakeholders in any formal discussions about your plans. Therefore, ownership and shared vision are the second part of the COMPASS model.

When teachers and others collaborate on instructional issues, their practice is more likely to change (Borko, 2004). Similarly, engaging all of the critical stakeholders at your school in efforts to school improvement will strengthen their collective commitment to the change (Garmston & Von Frank, 2012; Hord, 2009).

A while ago Ron and Howard Johnston from the University of South Florida began a study in four communities about increasing rigor in middle schools (Johnston & Williamson, 1998). As part of their research they asked parents, teachers, and students to think about a time when they felt challenged and involved in a rigorous activity. Everyone was asked to describe the experience, the feelings they had at the time of the experience, and the feelings they had as they recalled the experience.

From this study Ron and Howard found, not surprisingly, that teachers and parents held different perspectives on rigor. Often teachers described school rigor as doing more of what they were currently doing—more reading, more projects, more papers. Parents, on the other hand, said that rigor was doing fewer things but going more in depth, exploring the implications of ideas, synthesizing learning, and generating hypotheses. Obviously, not every parent or every teacher fit this description. But the patterns were clear. Not everyone agrees on what constitutes rigor.

It reminds us of an experience we had looking at several pieces of art. We couldn't agree on their meaning or on their value. One friend said he couldn't define art but he sure knew it when he saw it.

It's much the same with most school improvement initiatives. People often can't define it, or put a label on it, but they sure recognize it when it occurs.

Because of the varying perspectives about change, and programs and practices that support change, we've found that it is important to involve teachers, parents, and other appropriate stakeholders in any discussion. Be sure to include every group that has a role in the successful launch of any change. Chapter 6 will explore advocacy, one way to build support, in more detail.

Cultivating Ownership

Involving others in decisions about school improvement is essential. It is important to have a broad base of support from all of a school's key stakeholder groups—teachers and staff, parents, and community. Although there are clear benefits to building ownership, you will also want to consider how to overcome the barriers.

Facilitators and Barriers to Cultivating Ownership

Facilitators	Barriers
• Adequate time to meet; talk about improvement plans; plan, implement, and assess current efforts; lots of time may be required initially to get started; • Clear understanding of the areas/topics that the group can address; • Appropriate, ongoing professional development for all stakeholders, including conflict management and decision-making skills; • Accountability and responsibility of participants; • Availability of technical assistance; • Comfort and support of the principal.	• Little or no professional development provided about collaborative work; • Limits of decision-making authority are unclear or undefined; • Principal directs and tells rather than guides; • Only the principal or superintendent is held accountable for decisions; • Group does not have power to make "real" decisions and gets mired in unimportant details.

There is no formula for the perfect way to engage stakeholders in the discussion; however, authentic involvement around real tasks is important.

> **Sample Tasks**
> - Work to develop a shared vision for your school;
> - Invite teachers and parents to work together to look at data;
> - Interview parents and students about their perceptions of your school.

Most schools have groups that already provide input into decision-making—the School Improvement Team, a Principal's Advisory Committee, or a Professional Development Committee. You may want to involve these groups or you may want to create a special work group to guide your efforts.

Regardless, we have found that there are several important things that you should consider.

1. Who will be involved?
2. How will you form your team?
3. What contributions can individuals make? What is their level of expertise?
4. How will the team work together?

Determining Involvement

If people have a stake in the outcome of the decision and have some level of expertise, they should be involved. If an individual is indifferent to the outcome or has no expertise, no involvement is needed. Finally, if people have concerns about the outcome, but lack expertise, then they should have limited participation.

How to Determine Involvement	
Involve	Does this person have a stake in the outcome and have some level of expertise?
Don't Involve	Is this person indifferent to the outcome and have no expertise?
Limited Involvement	Does the person have concerns about the outcome but lacks expertise or is indifferent to the outcome?

Source: Adapted from Hoy and Tarter (2008)

Forming the Team and Getting Started

As you are determining the members of the team, it is also important to consider clarity of the task, how the group will be organized, and the decision-making process.

Checklist for Formation of Collaboration Teams

_____ Is the purpose clear? Is the role well defined?
_____ Is membership representative? Is membership appropriate to the task?
_____ Are there agreed upon norms for operation? For decision-making?
_____ Is there a mechanism to communicate with the larger school community? With other decision-making groups?
_____ What is the process for concluding the team's work?

Source: From Williamson and Blackburn (2016)

Reduce Isolation and Build Collaborative Relationships

We believe in the power of collaborative groups to positively impact schools. To assure greater success, a common base of information should guide every conversation. That means that family members are often working with teachers and principals on School Improvement Teams.

In some groups families and community members feel that teachers and principals have a greater voice in decisions and may have access to more information than they do. It is important to minimize these feelings by creating a culture where everyone has access to the same information. For example, everyone might be provided the same reading and then the group might spend time discussing the reading. Or you might ask everyone to review the same research from a recognized source like the College Board, or the Southern Regional Education Board (SREB).

Ron recently worked with a school near Chicago on a school improvement plan. A task force of teachers, parents, and administrators was organized to make recommendations. Central to their work was a review of data about the school.

The task force held several "data nights" where they met, examined the data together, discussed the implications, and rated the school's success. Small work groups continued the work with deeper analysis and recommending action steps.

These data nights helped assured that everyone had the same data, an opportunity to talk about its meaning, and contribute to the analysis.

The work around data helped to build trust among task force members and reduced the awkwardness that parents often feel when joining school improvement groups.

Developing a Vision

One of the most important things you can do as a leader is have a clear vision for your school. Michael Fullan (2015) identified a clear and compelling vision as one of the critical components of an effective school.

Beyond a general vision for your school, it is important that you and your teachers have a shared vision for what your school will look like as you work on school improvement.

Describing one's personal vision is not easy. Because it reflects our most intimate beliefs about life and about our work, preparing a statement of personal vision can be incredibly difficult. In their book on ethical leadership and decision-making, Joan Shapiro and Jacqueline Stefkovich (2016) describe work on a personal vision, or ethic, as one of the most important things a leader can do to be clear about what they value and about what is important in their school.

A Personal Vision

Your personal vision consists of the most fundamental beliefs you hold about life, about your work, and about relationships with people. A four-step process can be used to think about your own personal vision for your school.

> ### *Developing a Personal Vision*
>
> **Step 1:** Think about your school. Make a list of what you would like to achieve as you work on improvement. Describe what it looks like and feels like.
>
> **Step 2:** Consider the following things about what you have written—relationships, personal interests, and community. Examine each item in your list to ensure that it still fits.
>
> **Step 3:** Develop a list of priorities. Identify the most important. Once this is done, review the list and rank them from most to least important. Remove the least important. Re-rank if appropriate. Check for relevance with your earlier list. Eliminate any item that is not relevant.
>
> **Step 4:** Use the items from the first three steps to develop a personal vision statement. Review and edit the statement as often as needed until you believe it accurately reflects your commitment to your improvement plan.
>
> *Source:* Adapted from Williamson and Blackburn (2016)

Vision Letters

A personal vision is also important for teachers and others who work in your school. While the beginning of the school year is a good time to invite teachers to consider their own personal vision, it can occur at any time.

In her book on classroom motivation Barbara (2005) recommends having teachers write vision letters. The letters provide teachers with an opportunity to consider the sort of classroom they want to create.

For example, ask teachers to imagine that it is the last day of school and to write a letter or e-mail to another teacher describing the past year—all that students accomplished, the work in their classroom, ways they supported student learning. Then ask teachers to describe how they plan to achieve their vision.

One principal we worked with asks teachers to write a vision letter at the start of every school year. Several times during the year they are asked to look at the letter and think about their progress toward making the vision a reality. This principal reports that it is a "really helpful motivational tool."

Another way to use the vision letter is to have teachers write the letter to you as principal. You can then use the letter as a part of a conversation with each teacher about his or her vision of a more effective classroom and how it relates to your vision of a more effective school.

> ### A Vision Letter to the Principal
>
> Ask teachers to imagine that it is the last day of school, and the past year was the most successful year of their career. What happened in their classroom? What happened in the school? How did they grow personally and professionally?

Collaboration Connection

When you ask teachers to write a vision letter to you, consider asking parents and business leaders to do the same. Just be sure you ask a cross-section, rather than the ones who are always involved. Also, think about asking teachers to ask their students to write vision letters and share key information.

Possessing a clear and compelling personal vision is important but not sufficient. Effective principals recognize the importance of working with staff and community to develop, nurture, and sustain a strong, collectively held vision for their school.

Thinking About a Shared Vision

When asking people to think about their shared vision it can be helpful to involve participants in a thoughtful, yet engaging activity. One approach is to build on the vision letter activity. After teachers write their individual visions, have them meet in small groups, such as by grade level, in teams, or in subject area departments. Ask each group to discuss their letters and create a common vision for the small group. Finally, ask small groups to work together as a school faculty to write a shared vision for the school.

Another idea is the "View from a Hot Air Balloon." The principals we've worked with find this activity a fun way to launch the conversation about vision.

> Imagine you're hovering in a hot air balloon over your school and imagine it as good as it might be—what would you see, what would you feel, what would you hear?

At one school the principal used a two-step process. First, she asked teachers to describe what they would currently see and hear in their school. Then they were asked to imagine it was five years in the future and to describe what they would see and hear from their hot air balloon if their school was a result of their improvement plan.

Today	Five Years From Today

Creating or Recommitting to a School-Wide Vision

Skillful principals recognize the importance of working with their school community to develop, nurture, and sustain a collectively held vision for their school.

Every school we've visited has a mission or vision statement. Many, however, are out-of-date and rarely used to set goals and priorities, allocation of resources, or make decisions about school programs. Even the clearest statements need periodic review. A review allows you to adjust the mission and vision based on up-to-date information about students and their needs. A review also allows the staff "to recommit to the school's core values and beliefs" (Williamson & Blackburn, 2016).

Process for Developing a School Vision Statement

Activity 1: What are the things people are pleased with and frustrated about at this school? (Designed to get the issues on the table.)	
Activity 2: Invite the group to consider the values that should guide the school. You might ask, "As we begin planning for our future, what values are most important to you as we create our vision statement?" (Use of "I believe" statements focus on the important things.) *Note:* A helpful approach is to have the group read some common things. For example, information about developmental needs of students, future trends, information about recommendations for schools at that level. Often professional associations (NASSP, ASCD) have useful resources. Shared readings create a common base of information and are particularly useful to minimize the barriers between teachers and parents where parents often defer to teachers as the "experts."	
Activity 3: Ask the group to respond to the following: "Imagine it is the year 20XX. We have been able to operationalize our beliefs. What does our school look, sound, and feel like? Describe the vision." (Helps to identify the target the school will work towards.)	
Activity 4: In work groups develop a draft mission statement to be shared with the larger group. (Development of multiple models promotes discussion, clarification, and consensus building.)	
Activity 5: Share the drafts, ask questions, and seek clarification, and seek consensus on a statement. Plan to share it with the larger school community for feedback and comment.	

Source: From Williamson and Blackburn (2016)

Vision is one of the most important components of an effective school. Being clear about your personal vision and working with others to be clear about the vision for your school helps you and your faculty balance competing demands and make decisions based on your collective vision for your school.

District 102 outside of Chicago worked with Ron to develop their newly adopted vision statement for the middle grades.

District 102 Vision Statement

The vision of District 102's middle grades program is to prepare students intellectually and emotionally for personal and academic success in their school years and beyond. Our program's structure, organization, objectives, and goals will be based on the following values:

- A safe, supportive, and academically challenging learning environment that meets the unique needs of our adolescent learners;
- The development of all students to their full potential;
- Development of personal responsibility in all students;
- Respectful relationships among students, staff, families, and community; and
- Opportunities for exploration and expression for students across a broad range of disciplines.

Collaboration Connection

Building ownership is a natural opportunity for collaboration with parents, business partners, and students. Something as basic as involving them in discussions or asking them to complete a survey can help create a sense of ownership.

Seeking Agreement About Improvement Decisions

One struggle for many collaborative groups is how to make decisions. For many groups, the goal is to develop consensus but "absolute" consensus can be fleeting, or result in what feels like "watered-down" commitment.

It is essential that you engage everyone in the conversation. Seek to include every voice, particularly the missing voices of those who are often reluctant to speak out on issues. Welcome diverse ideas and give consideration to every one. It is critical to separate ideas from personalities and to be clear that once the faculty has decided on an approach, everyone is accountable for its implementation.

Although it is important to be clear about your personal vision for your school, you must also be committed to working together, and supporting, a mutually agreed-upon shared vision.

Avoid voting on issues if at all possible. Voting creates an adversarial tone, one of winners and losers. Work to seek agreement. One tool we've found helpful to move a group toward consensus is the "Fist to Five" (Fletcher, 2002). When using the "Fist to Five," ask every participant to raise their hand and indicate their level of support, from a closed fist (no support) to all five fingers (it's a great idea). The "Fist to Five" technique is an easy way to determine the opinion of each person. It is a visible indicator of support and can help a group seek common ground. Many groups we've worked with continue the process until everyone holds up a minimum of three fingers.

Fist to Five	
Fist	No support—"I need to talk more on the proposal and require changes to support it."
1 Finger	No support but won't block—"I still need to discuss some issues and I will suggest changes that should be made."
2 Fingers	Minimal support—"I am moderately comfortable with the idea but would like to discuss some minor things."
3 Fingers	Neutral—"I'm not in total agreement but feel comfortable to let this idea pass without further discussion."
4 Fingers	Solid Support—"I think it's a good idea and will work for it."
5 Fingers	Strong Support—"It's a great idea and I will be one of those working to implement it."

Source: Adapted from Adventure Associates (2009)

Consensus does not mean that everyone has to agree with a decision. It does, however, mean that everyone in the group can support the decision—they agree they can live with it.

Leadership in Action: Developing a Shared Vision

Ron recently with the staff in District 102 outside of Chicago. They were committed to strengthening their middle grades program and created a study group that included teachers, administrators, and parents to look at the program.

They quickly found that individuals held starkly different visions for the school and its program. A process was designed to create a collectively agreed-to statement of vision and several explicit supporting objectives. The group found that through their discussion about vision they developed greater understanding of the varying points of view.

Step 1: Discuss current conditions (strengths and opportunities).

Step 2: Use external facilitator to allow everyone to participate in the discussion.

Step 3: Identify areas of focus and provide evidence to support.

Step 4: Invite every member to suggest a statement of vision and supporting objectives and share with the facilitator who synthesizes for the group.

Step 5: Share all proposed statements of vision with every member and ask for their feedback and suggestions.

Step 6: Meet and discuss the proposed vision and each proposed objective, agreeing to keep, merge, or discard based on level of support.

Step 7: Agree on vision and supporting objectives.

Their adopted vision, shared earlier in this chapter, will serve to guide the further work at refining the program.

Final Thoughts

The most successful leaders are those that work with others to build a culture of continuous improvement. They recognize the importance of developing and nurturing a shared vision for their school and they value the participation of all stakeholders in decisions about their school's program.

Where Do I Begin?

If...	Then...
You need to think about how to build a foundation for ownership by stakeholders,	Review the barriers and facilitators to cultivating ownership.
You are ready to create teams to help with your initiative,	Check out the section on forming a team.
You are considering creating or adjusting your school's vision,	Look at how to create a personal vision and helping your staff develop individual and shared visions.
You are struggling with helping your teachers come to a consensus,	Consider the strategies in the collaborative decision-making section.

4

Managing Data

The third part of the COMPASS model is about appropriately managing data. Many principals are overwhelmed with the sheer amount of data they have and unsure how to turn it into useful information.

We want to be clear about what we mean by data. We're talking about all of the information you have, or you might collect, that will guide your work with teachers and families to improve your school. We believe that data is an important tool to guide decision-making, to measure success, and to monitor accountability. Our focus is on the use of data to help improve your school's program, not on data as an evaluative tool.

In this chapter, we'll suggest a four-step approach to the use of data to improve your school.

Four-Step Approach

1. Determine what you want to know;
2. Decide how you will collect the data;
3. Analyze the data/results;
4. Set priorities and goals based on the analysis.

Source: From Williamson and Blackburn (2016)

Step 1: Determine What You Want to Know

Be clear about what you want to know. Do you have questions about your school's program? About its success with students? About parent and community support? About instruction in your classrooms?

Clarity about what you want to know helps to clarify the data you might collect and analyze. In other words, what is your purpose for collecting and using data? That's an emphasis for each of the COMPASS tools because without a clear focus on why you are using the tool and how the tools support improvements in your school, they simply become activities—things to do.

The use of data should be linked to the shared vision (see Chapter 3: Ownership and Shared Vision). We suggest that rather than just saying, "We want to improve our school," you divide the task into smaller, more manageable chunks. For example, you might want to begin with a focus on one specific part of your program, one specific content area, or one specific grade.

We recognize that the almost universally accepted measure of school success is student scores on standardized tests, either national or state level. The most skillful principals, and most successful schools, are those that don't talk about raising test scores but rather focus on the things that teachers, principals, and families can impact like the curriculum, support structures for students, frequent assessment, and a willingness to monitor and adjust both curriculum and instruction as needed. When those things are addressed, results on standardized tests improve.

Possible Areas of Focus

- Expectations for students and their learning;
- Support for student learning;
- Assessments and demonstration of student learning;
- Engagement of families.

As you narrow your focus you may identify several areas of concern. We've found that the most successful schools are those in which improvement is a journey rather than an event. They select an initial area for improvement and put energy into it prior to moving to other areas.

There are many places where you might begin—curriculum, instruction, assessment, school environment. We've identified a sample of characteristics for expectations for students and their learning.

Sample Characteristics for Expectations for Students and Their Learning	
Curriculum	• Curriculum reflects new learning for students; • Curriculum is aligned with national and international standards; • Curriculum incorporates higher order thinking skills; • Curriculum focuses on application of knowledge; • Factual, knowledge-based information is applied; • Curriculum offers opportunities for students to see relevance to their own lives and to the real world.
Instruction	• Instruction offers opportunities for all students to engage in learning at high levels demonstrating that all students are expected to answer; • Instruction focuses on higher levels of questioning; • Review of basic information is streamlined and taught in a new manner; • Opportunities for application of learning are incorporated throughout the lesson; • Teacher wait time reflects the belief that all students are expected to answer.
Assessment	• Assessment of learning is varied and includes performance-based activities; • Assessments are structured so that students are given multiple opportunities for success; • Grading reflects a belief that it is mandatory to demonstrate learning.
School Environment	• Everyone involved in the school environment encourages students to perform at high levels; • Everyone involved in the school environment models continual learning; • Teachers and other staff support one another's initiatives to improve teaching and learning; • Shared goals focused on student learning are used to assess new ideas and practices.

This example is just a starting point. Every school will want to develop their own focus and work collaboratively with teachers, and families, to identify the goals for school improvement.

Step 2: Decide How You Will Collect Data

Once you've determined an area of focus you will want to think about the data you already have. Many schools routinely gather data of all sorts. Think about what you already have and how it might be used to guide your work. There's no need to gather data that's already available.

Data Frequently Available

- Student grades or test scores;
- Student, parent, and staff surveys;
- School climate data;
- Instructional practices data;
- Curriculum audit results;
- Report of alignment with state or national standards.

You may find that some of these data are helpful but that there are gaps. You may want additional, more targeted data to give you the information to support your work. We've identified four types of data you can collect. First, consider the types of data and determine which types of data will provide the information you need to develop your improvement plan, or measure your plan's success.

Types of Data

Demographic Data: These data describe the students and are most often used to understand the student learning data. It provides insight into equity among students.

Achievement and Learning Data: These data tell us what is going on in a school or district. They tell us what students learned and what they achieved. These data help us understand how students are achieving. Specific, disaggregated test item analyses provide insights into "what students got."

Instructional Process Data: These are the data that help you understand why students achieved at the level that they did. If reading scores

> are low, you might look at the type of reading students do, the time they spend on reading, the alignment of your reading program with state and local standards or benchmarks. These data also provide insights into why students in some classes learn and others may not. For example, teachers who participated in the recent training on the reading program achieve higher than students of teachers who did not participate.
>
> *Attitudinal Data:* These data tell you about how people feel about a program, about how they experience your school or district program. Attitudinal or perception data will reveal "how they feel or what they believe about it."
>
> *Source:* From Williamson & Blackburn (2016)

When considering the data you may need to collect, align with your purposes. We've found that it may be helpful to phrase your issue as a question. Then, consider what data you already have and what types of data you would like to collect. Again, you likely have data readily available to you. Examples include test score data, enrollment in classes, parent or student survey results, attendance patterns, and requests to drop/add classes and/or teachers.

Data Collection		
Purpose: Does the instruction at _____ School reflect a belief that all students can learn at high levels?		
Data Type	*Available Existing Data*	*Needed Data*
Demographic Data		
Achievement and Learning Data		
Instructional Process Data		
Attitudinal Data		

Ways to Collect Data

There are many different ways to collect data. It is helpful to include a mix of quantitative measures and qualitative measures. For example, student grades and test scores might be complemented by open-ended surveys or focus group conversations.

You may want to collect data on the curriculum that is in place, the instructional practices in your building, the assessments used to measure student learning, or the overall environment or school culture. Some of the tools we will suggest fit more than one category; others best fit just one area. Of most importance is that the data collection tool aligns with the area on which you are focusing.

Suggested Data Collection Strategies	
Curriculum	• Comparison of curriculum to outside benchmarks (see Chapter 5: Professional Development for process); • Review of curriculum maps and/or pacing guides; • Prioritization of vocabulary or standards internally and externally (need to put this process somewhere); • Analysis of test items rather than aggregate scores; • Comparison to NAEP scores; • Rubrics (self-assessment).
Instruction	• Classroom walkthroughs; • Lesson plan comparisons; • Student shadow studies; • Rubrics (self-assessment).
Assessment	• Comparison of levels of questioning; • Rubrics (self-assessment); • Variety of assessments including performance-based activities; • Analysis of test items.
Environment	• Governance plan; • School climate assessment; • Community involvement plans.

Data Collection Tools

There are several tools that may be used to collect information about current conditions. They include organizing an instructional walkthrough or instructional rounds, holding focus group discussions, looking at student work, conducting a lesson study, or using a rubric.

Instructional Walkthrough or Instructional Rounds

Another way to gather data about your school is to conduct an instructional walkthrough or instructional rounds. We do not suggest a quick tour of the school but rather a focused visit to your school's instructional areas to collect information about your school's program.

Recently, many of the teachers and principals we work with chuckle when we mention a walkthrough. Where a walkthrough is compulsory or part of an evaluation system, they are less successful.

When designed and implemented in a collaborative way, walkthroughs can be a useful tool for getting information about your school. Based on our experience in schools we suggest the following steps for a successful walkthrough.

Prior to Conducting the Walkthrough or Rounds

Establish a clear purpose for conducting a walkthrough. For example, it might be used to see how information from a recent Professional Development Workshop or Institute is used; gather data about implementation of a single instructional practice or learn about the presence of a variety of assessments.

Inform and prepare teachers. Regardless of the purpose, inform all teachers about, and prepare them for, the visit. They need to know who will be visiting, what data will be collected, and how the data will be shared and used following the walkthrough. Encourage teachers to conduct classes as they normally would, essentially ignoring the visitors and not interrupting routines. This is very important because a successful walkthrough collects data about current programs and practices. The walkthrough should not become a special event with specially designed lessons or activities.

Develop a plan for how observers will move throughout the school. This allows observers the opportunity to visit all instructional settings, rather than focusing on just one area. It may be appropriate to observe on more than one day and/or at various times throughout the day in the same classroom or instructional area.

Finally, identify the time needed to observe. Determine the amount of time for observation in each setting. The amount of time will depend on the observers' needs to get an accurate view of the instructional activity. Ensure that observers have the materials they need for recording their observations.

> ### Leadership in Action
>
> Area 10 of the Chicago Public Schools developed an instructional walkthrough process for collecting information about classroom instruction. Trinidad Liberto, Management Support Director for Area 10, described their "Instructional Rounds" process. Teams are created that include classroom teachers, a school coach, and administrator. Each team of three or four people visits classrooms for 30 minutes. During the visits team members scribe what the teacher and students are doing and saying and complete a "Data Gathering Form." The process is repeated in several classrooms. The data is analyzed to look for common findings and develop an action plan.

Conducting the Walkthrough or Rounds

Except in cases where classes may not be meeting, encourage observers to observe all instructional settings. Focus on the instructional practices present during the first few minutes of an observation. Data are recorded based on these initial observations.

While visiting classrooms, observers may want to talk with students. Responses from students can provide helpful information about your instructional program and expectations for students.

> ### Possible Questions of Students
> - What are you learning?
> - Why do you need to know this information?
> - What did you learn previously that helped you with this lesson?
> - How do you know your work is good enough?
> - If you want to make your work better, how do you know what to improve?
> - What is an example of something you've done where you had to work hard but also learned a lot?

After observers make their observations, they should move from the setting to a place of privacy and discreetly record the information. Assure that the recording of each observation is anonymous. Observers want to get a view of instructional practice across the school, not in any particular classroom.

Following the Walkthrough or Rounds

After gathering the data, provide an opportunity for all teachers to study the data and reflect on its meaning. Make all information collected available in an open and transparent way, one that invites conversation and discussion.

Engage teachers and other school personnel in conversation about the data, patterns that emerge, and meaning for their work together. Working with teacher leaders, develop a plan for this collaborative dialogue. Several formats might be considered, including:

- A discussion with the entire faculty;
- Talking with a team or the faculty at one grade level or in one content area.

Following the walkthrough, plan a debriefing with the observers. This meeting provides an opportunity to synthesize what was observed, to learn from other participants, and to deepen understanding of the instructional practices in your school. It also is a time to provide feedback to school personnel that will support continuous improvement.

Leadership in Action

At Aynor High School in Aynor, SC, teachers are able to participate in off-campus learning walks. Kelly Johnson, Curriculum Specialist, says that the walks provide an opportunity for teachers to gather information about practices in other schools and that the process is less threatening when conducted off campus.

Collaboration Connection

Incorporate students in your classroom walkthroughs. This can happen in two ways. First, informally ask students about the lesson either during your observation or at the end of class. Second, provide a simple three question exit slip for them to complete. Ask them: 1. What did you learn today? 2. What excited you about today's lesson? 3. If you were the teacher, what would you do differently?

Focus Group Meetings

Another strategy for gathering data about your school is to hold a series of focus group sessions with students, parents, teachers, or other interested people. A focus group is a group of individuals brought together to participate in a guided discussion about an issue of interest. The focus group can help you understand how members of the group experience the issue.

Focus group sessions consist of structured discussion and are generally most useful when conducted by an outside facilitator. This encourages participants to speak more freely and discuss difficult issues. The information that emerges should be scripted, analyzed for patterns and themes, and publicly reported and discussed.

When you arrange for a focus group, be clear about the purpose of the meeting. Most often, the purpose is to understand stakeholders' needs and to gather data about the current status of the school or a specific program. Explain that data will not be identified with an individual and that only themes will be reported, which allows for limited individual confidentiality. Prior to the meeting, develop and use a set of guiding questions to start the discussion. Finally, always follow up responses with requests for more detail and information. It is usually helpful to ask for an example that illustrates the thinking.

Examples of Guiding Questions or Probes for Focus Groups

General:

- Talk with me about your school. What's most important for me to know?
- What are the school's strengths? Its challenges?
- Describe your experience with this school.
- What qualities define a successful _____ school?
- Discuss this school's curriculum.

Specific:

- Talk about experiences you've had that you think are good teaching. What was going on? Why did you think it was "good?"
- When you feel really supported in your learning (or your student feels supported in his/her learning), what is happening?
- How would you describe this school's curriculum? What are examples of how the curriculum meets student needs?
- Discuss the expectations teachers have for student learning.
- What suggestions do you have for strengthening our instruction to assure a more engaging experience for students?
- If you could change one thing at this school, what would it be? Please explain.

Other Questions You Would Like to Ask:

Another way to obtain the students' view of instruction is to conduct focus groups or form a Principal's Advisory Group of students. If students trust you, and they believe that you want to listen to them, students will give you frank feedback about schools. One of our favorite questions to ask students is, "If you were in charge of the school, what would you change?"

Collaboration Connection

Focus groups should also include all stakeholders. You can gain much information with the answer to one question: if you were in charge of the school/classroom, what would you change?

Student Work

Finally, don't forget that a powerful source of information is student work. You might conduct a walkthrough with faculty to observe the school and student work or examine student work during grade-level, team, or department meetings. We'll also discuss this concept in more detail in Chapter 5: Professional Development.

Lesson Study

One way to gather data about the curriculum is to organize lesson study groups. Lesson study involves groups of teachers in a process to collaboratively develop lessons, teach the lesson, and then meet to discuss the lesson and its success and to plan for follow-up activities. The goal is to work together to develop, test, and refine instructional activities in classrooms. For example, the focus might be on expectations for students or opportunities to revise and resubmit student work.

Researchers from the University of Wyoming identified several positive benefits. They include the collaborative nature of the work, the sustained and ongoing process, and how the way the teacher voice is honored in the work. The model recognizes that a prescriptive "top-down" approach to school reform has not been effective.

Student Shadow Study

An effective way to gather information on the curricular and instructional experiences of students is to conduct a shadow study. Shadow studies involve selecting students at random and following them throughout their day.

The protocol, originally developed by the NASSP, suggests charting the experience of students at five- to seven-minute intervals. This allows the observer to see the ebb and flow of activities during the day. Spending the entire day with a student and documenting his or her experience provides interesting insights into the student experience. Of course, students quickly figure out that something is going on. The best approach is to talk with the student and assure him or her that you are not gathering information about them to report to the office.

Shadow Study Observation Form

Time	Specific Behavior (Five- to Seven-Minute Intervals)	Comments and Impressions

After gathering the data, the information can be used as a springboard to launch conversations at the faculty, grade, or departmental level about the experience of students. The patterns that emerge across students and across classrooms can provide helpful guidance to improve instructional quality.

In *Rigor Is Not a Four-Letter Word* (2012), Barbara shares her experience with a student responding to this question. The school had good test scores and used those scores to place students in tracked classes. The principal and faculty believed that all classes were of high quality and were sufficiently challenging for each student. Gabrielle, a sixth grader in the school, responded, "For people who don't understand as much. . . [they should] be in higher-level classes to understand more [because] if they already don't know much, you don't want to teach them to not know much over and over."

The principal and teachers were taken aback. They had no idea that students in the school viewed the lower-level classes as less challenging. The feedback from Gabrielle prompted them to reevaluate their curriculum and instruction.

Use a Rubric

An effective way to gather data about how teachers or other members of the school community think your school is doing is through the use of rubrics. First, you need a clear, detailed rubric that is customized to the specific area or areas you want to assess. Next, introduce the rubric categories to your faculty. You might want to organize teachers into small groups and ask them to describe what each item would look like in a classroom. Ask them to compare their perspectives with a standard set of descriptors, such as the ones in this sample.

Sample Rubric Related to Instruction

Instruction: The school staff utilizes a range of instructional strategies that focus on student success and high expectations for the learning of all students.

At this school we...	Maintain high expectations for learning	Include support and scaffolding in classroom instruction
High	Teachers act consistently on the unwavering belief that each student can learn, will learn, and it is in their power to help them do so.	Teachers regularly provide the support and scaffolding each student needs to ensure their success. The support is customized for each student and affirms the belief that students are not allowed to not learn.
Medium	Teachers believe that each student can learn and that they can help them do so. They sometimes act on those beliefs or act on those beliefs with some students.	Teachers provide support and scaffolding for students to ensure their success. The support is customized for each student some times. At times, optional extra help is provided.
Low	Teachers are working to understand what it means that each student can learn, will learn, and they can help them do so.	Teachers sometimes provide support and scaffolding. The support is general and built into the regular lesson. At times, optional extra help is provided.

Finally, ask each member of your faculty to assess the school in each category, using the descriptors as a guide. However, it's also important to ask them to provide evidence for the ranking they choose. This will provide more detailed information for follow-up discussions.

Descriptor	*Ranking*	*Evidence*
Maintain high expectations for learning		
Include support and scaffolding in classroom instruction		

One way to use a rubric is for an internal self-assessment. But internal assessments are often inflated, may not accurately reflect what is really going on, or lack credibility with parents and other external groups.

Another way to use a rubric is to have someone knowledgeable about your school improvement focus. They can use an established rubric to measure your school's current status and progress at improvement. Assessments conducted by experts in the area, external to the school, frequently have much greater credibility and can help to identify a school improvement agenda.

Collect Your Data

Next, collect data. You may have decided to use readily available data and/or determined ways to gather local data about your focus area. Collected data should align with the data analysis questions. A crosswalk (see below) provides a visual tool to track the appropriate data to match each question.

Data Crosswalk			
Data Analysis Question	Does the instruction at _____ School reflect a belief that every student is expected to learn at high levels?	Are teachers persistent in supporting student learning?	Are students engaged in instructional activities that use high-order thinking?
Demographic Data			
Achievement and Learning Data			
Tracking Processes Data			
Attitudinal Data			

Step 3: Analyze the Data/Results

As you begin to analyze your data, be sure to involve all constituents in the process, which we discussed in Chapter 3: Ownership and Shared Vision. During analysis it's important to keep an open mind rather than pre-determining the results. Otherwise, you may not see the full picture. First, analyze the information provided by each data source.

Data Source Analysis		
Data Source:		
Areas of Strength	Areas for Potential Growth	Areas That Need More Information

Then, look for patterns across multiple data points. This will allow you to prioritize action steps in areas that need the most work. You may find that you don't have enough data to select an area of focus. If so, consider how you might gather additional data.

Data Pattern Analysis			
Areas of Strength			
Focus Area	Data Source 1	Data Source 2	Data Source 3
Areas for Potential Growth			
Focus Area	Data Source 1	Data Source 2	Data Source 3
Areas That Need More Information			
Focus	Data Source 1	Data Source 2	Data Source 3

Many schools try to work on too many things at the same time. This dissipates the energy of teachers and administrators and may not provide the improvement you seek. A thorough pattern analysis will help you prioritize areas for improvement. Although you will want to involve teachers in the data analysis process, at some point the data must be shared with a larger audience, whether that is all teachers, or stakeholder groups. Planning thoughtfully and purposefully for the discussion is foundational for positive growth. One of the lessons we've learned about presenting and using data is the importance of presenting data in a non-threatening way in order to ensure purposeful engagement. Rather than discussing areas of concern, we've termed it areas for potential growth.

Force Field Analysis

A force field analysis is a tool for diagnosing situations, and it can provide clear guidelines for action. The process works well with small as well as large groups and provides an opportunity to examine both facilitators and inhibitors of change.

To do so, consider both driving forces and restraining forces that are helping or hurting your efforts to improve your school. Driving forces are those forces affecting a situation that are pushing in a particular direction; they tend to initiate a change and keep it going. Restraining forces are forces acting to restrain or decrease the driving forces.

Sample Driving Forces	Sample Restraining Forces
• Data about student learning; • Demographic data; • Number of students who drop out of college after graduating from your high school; • Data from local employers about numbers of new employees who need basic retraining.	• Belief that some students can't achieve at high levels; • Pressure from parents for high grades or rigid instructional groups; • Apathy; • Contractual issues; • Costs of an innovation.

Using the Force Field Analysis

A force field analysis allows you to look at all the forces for or against your initiative. It helps you plan for or reduce the impact of the opposing forces and strengthen and reinforce the supporting forces.

In order to conduct a force field analysis, state the problem or desired state in clear, concrete terms. Next, discuss and identify the factors that are working for and against the desired state.

Factors Working For	Factors Working Against

Third, review and clarify each factor. Once you agree on the list of factors, determine the strength of each factor. For example, assign a score to each force, from 1 (weak) to 5 (strong) or high, medium, or low. Finally, discuss the factors and their scores to identify appropriate next steps. Those factors working against the desired state may become the focus of plans of action. This information will help you set your priorities and goals.

Step 4: Set Priorities and Goals

The fourth data management step is to work with your School Improvement Team or other collaborative group to determine priorities based on your area of focus and your analysis of data.

Once you have determined your priorities, goals, or area of focus, study and select strategies that will allow you to address the area of focus. This is a pivotal point. Too often, we gather and analyze data, set goals, but then do not use that information to make decisions on an ongoing basis. We've developed an action planning process for the use of data.

> **Action Planning Process**
>
> *Data Source(s)*
>
> - Areas for potential growth;
> - Ways to measure success;
> - Action steps.

Using your pattern analysis, note the data sources you used. Next, identify the area for potential growth, such as incorporating more activities in which each student is required to demonstrate learning. Third, design a specific way to track success. How will everyone know if they are making progress toward the goal? What does success look like? Finally, detail the specific action steps that are needed to accomplish the goal.

Action Plan Template for Use of Data		
Data Source(s)		
Area for Potential Growth	*Indicators for Tracking Success*	*Action Steps*

Leadership in Action

Park Junior High School in suburban Chicago recently began to look at its middle grades program, grades six–eight. Part of the process was to clarify the program's mission and vision and identify specific measurable objectives that would indicate the program's success in accomplishing its mission.

A Middle Grades Task Force of teachers, parents, and administrators was created to guide the process. With the help of an external evaluator knowledgeable in middle grades programs, they rewrote their vision and discussed supporting objectives. More importantly the group identified more than 20 different sources of data that could be used to help identify action steps.

The Task Force held several different "data nights" where they examined the data, discussed its implications, and rated the program's current success in the area. Small work groups met to continue the analysis and suggest appropriate next steps.

Following this data review the district developed an action plan that would strengthen the current program and support its continued improvement.

Final Thoughts

Gathering and using data to guide decisions about school improvement is important. Be cautious about simply gathering data. The value of data is in its analysis and use to help select improvement strategies and monitor your progress meeting your improvement goals.

Leaders who are most successful use data routinely to guide their work, but they recognize that it is vitally important to involve teachers, staff, and families in both the collection and use of the data.

Where Do I Begin?

If...	Then...
You want a basic process to follow,	Review the four-step approach to working with data.
You aren't sure of the variety of data sources,	Look at the frequently available data and types of data charts.
You'd like to get feedback from stakeholders during small-group meetings,	Check out the section on focus groups.
You are finding there are competing forces about moving forward or backward toward your school's initiative,	Think about using the force field analysis tool.

5

Professional Development

Effective professional development is an essential support for any school improvement plan. Traditionally, professional development has included large group activities like workshops, seminars, courses, or conferences. These types of activities have varied in terms of effectiveness, and we've come to recognize that job-embedded and personalized professional development is more effective. This model provides a greater variety of activities and options for professional learning.

Contemporary professional development includes peer coaching, collaborative work teams, study groups, action research teams, mentoring, and other activities that support a teacher-leadership approach.

Contemporary Professional Learning Models

According to *Learning Forward* (2019), a national organization committed to improving professional learning (www.learningforward.org), contemporary professional development should have three characteristics:

1. Results driven;
2. Standards based;
3. Job embedded.

Professional development should focus on clear results and promote the growth and learning of teachers and administrators. Activities should be based on standards, and should be thoroughly woven into the job, rather than simply being an activity that is done as an "extra," possibly outside of work hours or on staff development days.

Lessons From Award-Winning Schools

Barbara's research examining staff development in schools that won the US Department of Education's Award for Staff Development (Blackburn, 2000) identified several characteristics. Effective staff development had a clear purpose linked to research, student data, and goals. Teachers were accountable for using the professional development in their classrooms to impact student learning. There was an emphasis on developing a common, shared language to talk about issues. Decisions about professional development were made with teacher input, and professional development incorporated relevant, practical, hands-on activities. Finally, school leaders supported professional development and it took place in a positive, collegial atmosphere.

Each of these elements is critical to a successful professional development program. However, it is important to give more than surface attention to these elements. For example, asking teachers to be accountable for professional development is more than requiring teachers to attend a session or develop a strategy to use in a lesson. Instead, ask teachers to show you samples of student work that match recommended strategies or to provide a video of a lesson in which the professional development strategy is implemented.

The first step to effective professional development is to assess what you are already doing. Use the rating scale to determine the status of your efforts, then list specific evidence to support your rating.

Assess Your Professional Development Efforts

Rate the status of your professional development using this scale:	
1—Needs More Work	3—Underway but still working on it
2—Getting Started	4—Doing Very Well
Characteristic Rating	**Evidence**
1. Our professional development is guided by a clear purpose linked to research, data about student learning, and clearly identified goals and needs.	
2. Following professional development, we're held accountable for using the things we've learned in our classrooms to impact student learning.	
3. We're developing a common, shared language.	
4. Decision-making about professional development includes teacher input.	
5. Our professional development incorporates relevant, practical, hands-on activities.	
6. We integrate initial professional development with opportunities for follow-up and application.	
7. Our leaders support professional development and it occurs in a positive, collegial atmosphere.	
8. We move beyond traditional staff development methods to include options such as inquiry action research projects, book study groups, mentoring, peer coaching, and collaborative work teams.	

How Do These Elements Support Your School Improvement Goals?

Once you have assessed what you are doing, determine how you want to build on your strengths, and improve upon your weaknesses with new opportunities.

Refining Your Professional Development

Area	Strengths	Opportunities
Clear purpose: What component of your plan do we want to improve? Is it justified by the data? Does the research support the plan?		
Accountability: How will the PD be used to support improved student learning? How will you know students benefit? What will you see in classrooms?		
Common, shared language: How will you work to develop and use a shared language to talk about your work?		
Shared decision-making: How will teachers be authentically involved in decisions about professional development?		

Area	Strengths	Opportunities
Relevant, practical, hands-on activities: Are the activities relevant to teachers? Are participants able to interact to increase engagement?		
Opportunity for follow-up and application: How will you incorporate the learning after the training? Does each participant need to develop an action plan? How will you follow up with teachers?		
Leadership and a positive, collegial atmosphere: Who provides leadership for your professional development plan? How will you use some of your current meeting time for professional development? How will you create a positive, collegial, and supportive atmosphere?		

Professional Learning Communities

Many schools use professional learning communities as a tool for improved professional learning. The term has become so commonplace it is used to describe almost any sort of collaborative work.

The professional community of learners, originally suggested by Astuto and colleagues (1993) and then promoted by DuFour et al. (2006), reflects the commitment of teachers and administrators who continuously seek to learn and grow professionally and then act on what they learn. The goal is to improve student learning by improving effectiveness. Effective learning communities have three defining characteristics.

> **Defining Characteristics of PLCs**
>
> 1. They focus on ensuring that students learn;
> 2. They create a culture of collaboration;
> 3. They focus on results (whatever it takes).

Benefits and Challenges of PLCs—Many schools find professional learning communities a valuable way to support school improvement. However, there are also challenges. There are four major reasons PLCs fail.

> **Reasons PLCs Fail**
>
> 1. Lack of meaningful collaboration;
> 2. Climate of competition rather than cooperation;
> 3. Ineffective structures, whether that is insufficient time for meetings or a lack of coherent time or agenda during meetings;
> 4. Lack of ownership.

Assess Your Readiness

As always, you should start by assessing your current status. Here's a short tool to help you think about your role as a leader and how you support your professional learning communities.

Professional Learning Communities: Assess Your Own Dispositions

Use this scale to rate your dispositions about professional learning communities:	
1—Strongly Disagree	3—Agree
2—Disagree	4—Strongly Agree

Rating	
1. I expect the professional staff at this school to use their talents and knowledge to help one another improve as teachers.	
2. I encourage teachers to learn new ideas and use them in the classroom.	
3. It is important to provide time and resources for teachers to do their best work.	
4. I recognize and appreciate good teaching at my school.	
5. I promote honest, open communication among the staff at this school.	
6. As the leader of this school, I ask my teachers to be involved in analyzing student learning data, setting goals, and monitoring our success.	
7. I ask teachers to use a research base to inform our work with students and with one another.	
8. I'm comfortable adopting new practices even if they may not be successful the first time.	
What are the top three areas for improvement for you? What is one step you could take to improve each?	

You can also assess the readiness level of your teachers.

Teacher's Readiness to Participate in a PLC		
Scale: 3—Ready to Go; 2—Willing to Try; 1—I'd Rather Work on My Own		
Characteristic	Assessment	Examples
I believe working together is better than working alone.		
I like to share my ideas and work with other teachers.		
I believe that I can improve with input from others.		
I'm open to constructive criticism.		
I'm willing to participate in collaborative conversations that are designed to improve, not criticize.		

Collaborative Professional Development Activities

There are many different ways to organize professional learning groups. Like most things, each has advantages and disadvantages. It is important to select a strategy that fits your goal, allows you to maintain momentum on achieving your vision, and one that matches available resources.

This section will describe seven approaches that we've found useful: book study groups, looking at student work, feedback loops, learning walks, charrettes, unconferences, and technology-based options.

Book Study

A good way to engage people in their own professional learning is to organize a book study group. At some schools, every teacher is asked to read the same book and work in small groups to discuss the book and its implications for practice. At other schools, teachers may choose from several books and join colleagues who selected the same book for their discussion.

Some schools use technology for book study groups. For example, at Brookings-Harbor High School in Oregon, book study was a part of their annual professional development plan. Rather than meet in small groups on campus where one or two people might dominate the discussion, they used Moodle (http://mooodle.org), open-source software that is free and readily available online. With Moodle it is possible to create small discussion groups using threaded discussions. Each member of the groups can make comments, and respond to the comments of others. They report that not only did participation increase but the quality of the discussion improved. One of the benefits is that teachers were able to participate any time of the day, at their convenience. That provided for more engaging and thoughtful discussion.

Book Study Protocol

- Membership should be voluntary, but inclusive.
- Decide a meeting schedule, meeting place, length of book to be read, and what will happen after the book is read. It is recommended that meetings last no more than one hour and be held at a consistent time and place.
- Select a responsible facilitator to keep the group on task and help manage the meetings.
- Select a book with a clear objective in mind. For example, use *Motivating Struggling Learners: 10 Strategies for Student Success* to address issues related to students who lack motivation about learning.
- Conversation is important in a book study. Members of the group share insights, ask questions about the text, and learn from others. It is important to talk about how the ideas can be applied directly in the classroom and how to overcome any potential obstacles.
- Journaling is a useful way for members to think about their reading and reflect on how it might be used.

Plan for Organizing a Book Study

How will we determine membership?	
What is our meeting schedule?	
Who will be the facilitator?	
What book(s) will we use?	
How will we ensure conversation?	
How will we use journaling?	

Looking at Student Work

A powerful way to improve your school's instructional program is to look at authentic student work. In many schools, teams of teachers, either at the departmental, course, or grade level, examine student work as a way to clarify their own standards for that work, to strengthen common expectations for students, or to align curriculum across faculty.

Because looking at student work significantly alters the norms of a school, it necessitates a climate where teachers are comfortable sharing their work and revealing artifacts about their classroom practice. The Annenberg Institute for School Reform suggests several preliminary steps.

Looking at Student Work Protocol

- Talk together about the process and how to ensure it is not evaluative.
- Identify ways to gather relevant contextual information (e.g., copy of assignment, scoring guide or rubric).
- Select a protocol or guideline for the conversation that promotes discussion and interaction. See www.weteachnyc.org/resources/collection/protocols-looking-student-work/ for examples of different protocols.
- Agree on how to select work samples.
- Establish a system for providing and receiving feedback that is constructive.

Here's a short planning tool for planning to look at student work.

Planning to Look at Student Work

What is our process? How can we assure it is not evaluative?	
What materials and resources do we need to collect? Who is responsible for each?	
What protocol or guidelines will we use?	
How will we select work samples?	
What is our system for constructive feedback?	

Collaboration Connection

You may choose to ask students questions prior to the teacher discussion. For example, if you ask questions such as "Was this assignment easy or hard? If so, what parts? Was there something in particular you didn't understand? If so, what?", then you can use that information to inform the conversation with teachers.

Feedback Loops

We've found that there are times when teachers have different expectations for how to implement specific state and national standards. Even though teachers are using the same standards and they may have different expectations for student learning related to the standards, it's also important to develop a plan for greater consistency. In this case, *The Protocol for a Conversation About Expectations* is a step-by-step guide to this process.

> **Protocol for a Conversation About Expectations**
>
> **Step 1:** Gather copies of a standard assignment, such as a short essay, completed by students. Be sure to have copies from several teachers.
> **Step 2:** Share copies of the assignment with the group and ask everyone to assess it.
> **Step 3:** Meet to discuss the results. Use prompts to guide the discussion. For example, "How do you determine quality?", "What do you consider in a quality assignment?," or "What do you expect students to know in order to complete this assignment?"
> **Step 4:** You may want to extend the conversation to other grade levels. Discussion prompts might include, "What are some areas that students struggle with?" or "What do you expect students to know before they come into your class?"

One strategy Barbara uses with teachers is a feedback loop. This can work with a variety of strategies we have recommended, including Looking at Student Work and Developing Consistent Expectations.

In a feedback loop, teachers start with an individual reflection on a work sample, whether it is on a lesson plan, assignment, sample of student work, or a video. Using a reflective guide, each teacher reviews the product individually.

Reflective Guide	
Students' Instructional Needs	
What are the aspects of the product (lesson plan, assignment, work sample, video) that you believe meet the instructional needs of your students?	
What are the aspects of the product (lesson plan, assignment, work sample, video) that you believe need to be adjusted to meet the instructional needs of your students?	

Reflective Guide	
Students' Developmental Needs	
What are the aspects of the products that meet the developmental needs of your students?	
What are the aspects of the products that need to be adjusted to meet the developmental needs of your students?	
Match With Standards	
What are the aspects of the product that you believe match the standards, assessments, and preparation for the next grade level, college, or career?	
What are the aspects of the product that you believe need to be adjusted to match the standards, assessments, and preparation for the next grade level, college, or career?	
Other Notes	
Questions	

Following the individual reflection, teachers meet in pairs or small groups, whether by grade level, interdisciplinary team, or subject area departments. Teachers share the product, as well as their reflections, and ask for input from the group.

Group Summary Sheet		
Instructional Needs	**Developmental Needs**	**Standards/Challenge**
Other Thoughts or Questions		

Finally, the individual teacher or the group of teachers broadens their audience for feedback. You may include teachers from the grade level below the grade level with the product, as well as the grade level above the product, using the same group summary guide. We find that broadening the grade level can inform teachers' practice in a new and different way.

For example, Barbara worked with one group of fifth grade teachers who were trying to determine if they needed to adjust their math instruction. The grade level agreed that the instruction was appropriate, although challenging for their students. However, when meeting with the fourth grade teachers, they discovered that the standards in question were introduced in fourth grade, so students should have entered fifth grade with some level of understanding. Then, sixth grade teachers noted that, although students began sixth grade with a basic understanding of the particular math concepts, there were some missing applications students should have been taught. The feedback from the other grade levels was critical to the fifth grade teachers' understanding of needed adjustments.

Learning Walks

A learning walk is a form of instructional walkthrough, but they are typically organized and led by teachers. Learning walks are not evaluative. They are not designed for individual feedback, but instead help participants learn about instruction and identify areas of strength as well as need.

Learning walks provide a "snapshot" of the instructional program at your school. Since participants are in classrooms for only a short time, they should not draw conclusions about individual teachers or classes.

One school in Los Angeles held learning walks each month. Groups of teachers conducted the walks looking for evidence of the use of research-based instructional practices described in *Classroom Instruction That Works: Research-Based Strategies for Increasing Student Achievement (2nd ed.)* (Dean, Hubbell, Pitler, & Stone, 2012). Learning Walks provides guidelines for the learning walk process.

Learning Walks

1. Work with your staff to identify the purpose of the learning walk.
2. Determine the process including length of classroom visits as well as what will occur during the visits. Develop and use a consistent tool for participants to use to record their observations and collect data.
3. Inform staff when the learning walks will occur.
4. Conduct a pre-walk orientation for those participating.
5. Conduct the learning walk and spend no more than five minutes in each classroom. Depending on the lesson, talk with the teacher and students, look at student work, and examine the organization of the classroom.
6. Immediately after the walk, ask participants to meet and talk about the information they gathered and how to share it with the faculty. They may develop questions that they would ask to learn more about what is occurring.
7. Develop a plan for sharing the information and for using it to guide your continued school improvement work.

Collaboration Connection

Short student conversations can also add to your understanding of what is happening during your observation. Gear your specific questions to the purpose of the learning walk.

Charrettes

A "charrette" is a set of agreed-upon guidelines for talking with colleagues about an issue. The conversation tends to be more trusting and more substantive because everyone knows the guidelines in advance. Charrettes are often used to improve the work while the work is in progress and are not to be used as an evaluative tool. The Charrette Protocol below describes the process.

Charrette Protocol

1. A group or an individual from the group requests a charrette when they want others to help them resolve an issue. Often they are at a "sticking point" and the conversation will help them move forward.
2. Another small group is invited to look at the work and a facilitator is used to moderate the discussion.
3. The requesting group or individual presents its work and states what they need or want from the discussion. The conversation is focused by this presentation.
4. The invited group discusses the issue and the requesting group listens and takes notes. The emphasis is on improving the work, which now belongs to the entire group. "We're in this together" characterizes the discussion.
5. Once the requesting group gets what it needs, it stops the process, summarizes what was learned, thanks participants, and returns to their work.

Source: Adapted from "Charrette Protocol," written by Kathy Juarez and available on the *School Reform Initiative* website

---

Charrettes work best with a facilitator to guide the discussion and monitor the work of the group. We've provided an excerpt of a typical charrette discussion. Additional information about the charrette is available at http://schoolreforminitiative.org/doc/charrette.pdf.

Example of a Charrette Discussion

Opening: *Thank you for meeting with me today. We've been asked to get a brief update on the work of the task force looking at providing additional support for students. The group is having difficulty resolving some of the logistical issues related to their recommendations and want our assistance.*

Person/Group Presents Issue: *We have many ideas about how to provide students with additional support both during the school day and beyond. One of the things we haven't resolved is how to assure that teachers will use the strategies and participate in our lunchtime and after school activities.*

> **Discussion:** *Thank you. What questions of clarification does the group have for the task force? Discuss the issue and let's generate several ideas that the task force can use as they continue to work on their recommendations.*
>
> **Conclusion:** A member of the task force might say, *Thank you for your suggestions. They helped us clarify the issues and think about the advantages and disadvantages of our plan. We'll continue to work on the issue and share our recommendations with the faculty.*

Unconferences

Recently, unconferences, which are also called Ed Camps, Foo Camps, barcamps, and Open Space Technology, have become popular. You will find purists who prefer one term to another, but each is participant driven, both in content development and the sharing of content. In other words, participants identify questions or themes of interest, and other participants lead a discussion of the material. Generally, these activities have an organizing topic or overarching theme, but some, especially Foo Camps and barcamps, do not.

> ### Characteristics of Unconferences
>
> Focus on interaction of participants;
> Leaders facilitate and/or moderate conversations rather than presenting;
> Peer-to-peer interaction is emphasized;
> Learning is self-driven and self-organized;
> Most important issues of participants tend to rise to the top;
> Issue is addressed by the most capable participant.

Unconferences can occur locally, or on a regional, national, or international level. They also can be short, such as a one-hour block for a PLC, or for several days at a national conference. Their use has increased and is beneficial in certain circumstances where distance or resources may be an issue. As always, be clear about the purpose of professional development. If it matches, then it is an effective option.

Technology-Based Options

Although we have already mentioned one way to incorporate technology into your professional development, we wanted to share other ways that districts are using technology.

Many schools use GoogleDocs to share important information. As one principal told Barbara, "this ensures everyone has access to the information, and it frees up meeting time for activities related to instruction."

Next, the use of videos can enhance professional development. Sites such as *The Teaching Channel* provide informational videos, but also provide classroom demonstrations. These allow your teachers to watch and critique teaching without visiting an actual classroom. Barbara regularly uses videos with principals so they can practice their observational skills related to instruction.

Sample Sites for Teaching Videos

Teaching Channel (www.teachingchannel.org);
Engage NY (www.engageny.org/video-library);
America Achieves (http://commoncore.americaachieves.org);
Teachers Network (www.teachersnetwork.org/videos/);
Inside Mathematics (www.insidemathematics.org/classroom-videos);
WatchKnowLearn (www.watchknowlearn.org).

With the popularity of social media sites, many districts take advantage of that interest. One strategy is to use Twitter Chats. Chatham County, North Carolina sets a regular time for their chats, and they invite experts in the designated focus area to participate. This allows teachers to interact and ask more questions than in the traditional model of training.

Monique Flickinger, Director of Instructional Technology of Poudre Schools in Colorado, shares how her district uses Facebook.

> We created a Facebook account, TeachTechPSD, where we post weekly updates on new technology, pictures of classes using tech and other fun things we are learning about. When teachers come to training with us, we ask them to "like" us so that, when they check their own accounts, they will quickly see what we are up to.

Finally, the use of webinars has increased in popularity in recent years. Although many of these online presentations are scheduled at certain times, many are available on demand, particularly if you register for them in advance. Webinars are available from state and national organizations, as well as commercial groups. Although some have a fee, many do not. The Texas Association for Elementary Principals and Supervisors (TEPSA) has been offering traditional webinars for years. However, in 2018, they adjusted and began offering *Fast 15* on demand, in which the leader or author presents for 15 minutes in a conversational style. They are finding these are popular, in part because busy leaders can choose their own time for a 15-minute professional development on timely topics.

PRESS Forward Model for Planning Professional Development

Each of the strategies we've shared can make a positive difference in your school. You will need to determine which approaches may be most effective in your situation, and you'll likely need to customize them to your setting. For example, for the curriculum alignment activity, high school teachers tend to meet in departments, middle schools in teams, and elementary schools by grade levels. However, it is critical to start with a plan that incorporates the elements of effective professional development: focused on results, job embedded, and standards based.

We've developed the PRESS Forward Model for Planning Professional Development. You design a plan that has a clear purpose, is related and connected to other aspects of your school community, has a set of clear outcomes and action steps, and describes the support that is needed to be successful.

Our plan is cyclical, with benchmarks built into each stage of the process so that you can reflect on your successes and refine your plan before you move forward. The template for PRESS Forward provides a blank form for your use.

PRESS Forward Model for Planning Professional Development

PRESS Forward	
Purpose	Why are we doing professional development on this topic?
Relationships and Connections	How does this topic relate to our mission, our goals, and the needs of our students? How does it connect with other initiatives in our school?
Expected Outcomes	If the professional development is effective, what changes will we see related to teachers' practice and student learning?
Steps to Take	What are the specific action steps we need to take to accomplish our goals? What is the timeline for each step?
Support Needed	What types of support do we need to accomplish each step? What material resources are necessary?
Forward	After a stage of implementation, take time to reflect, refine your plan, and move forward with next steps.

Template for PRESS Forward

PRESS Forward	
Purpose	
Relationships and Connections	
Expected Outcomes	
Steps to Take	
Support Needed	
Forward	

Final Thoughts

The most successful schools are those that are committed to the continued professional growth and development of everyone on the staff. They recognize the importance of investing in people and assuring that they have the knowledge and skills needed for continued success. Professional learning communities and other collaborative structures provide a mechanism for teachers, principals, and other staff to make the improvement of student learning a priority.

One of the most valuable tools you can use to achieve your vision of a more effective school is a focused, standards-based, high-quality professional development program. Assess where you are, then build a successful plan.

Where Do I Begin?

If...	Then...
You need to assess your current efforts,	Use the professional development assessment, the PLC leadership assessment, and the teacher PLC assessment.
You are looking for an effective strategy for your PLCs,	Begin with book study groups, looking at student work, feedback loops, learning walks, and charrettes.
You are looking to enhance technology options,	Check out the technology section and the information about Unconferences.
You are reading to build a plan,	Start with PRESS Forward.

6

Advocacy

Everyone's an advocate whether we recognize it or not. School leaders are natural advocates always advocating for their school and the resources and programs to improve the educational experience of their students. It is one of a leader's most important roles.

Advocacy is what you do when you are actively promoting a cause like incorporating literacy one-to-one technology in your school. It is often compared to public relations. But advocacy is more than public relations. When a leader advocates for their program, they are committed to providing information to stakeholder groups that will build support for their vision. They recognize the importance of building networks and alliances that will support their efforts.

Advocacy is a way to effectively press for change. It is also the foundation of our democracy and a process that allows ordinary people to shape and influence policy at all levels of the system. Identifying priorities, crafting a strategy, taking action, and achieving results are critical steps to finding one's voice, making oneself heard, and shaping one's future.

Self-Assess Your Advocacy Skills

You may be unsure about your advocacy skills. Throughout this chapter, we'll provide specific tools that can help you. However, there are some key characteristics that are also important. Use the checklist below to assess your current skills.

Self-Assess Your Advocacy Skills

	I already do this	I need to work on this
I know the focus of our school and can explain it to others.		
I regularly share information about our school through a variety of sources, such as word of mouth, meetings, promotional materials, and online outlets.		
I can effectively communicate my message through clear, concise information and stories about my school.		
I can frame issues to match my audience.		
We have an advocacy plan for our school.		
I have a network of supporters to help me advocate for our school.		
I am comfortable using technology and social media to advocate for my school.		
I have a set of advocacy tools, including sound bites, success stories, elevator talks, and one-page fact sheets.		

Design an Advocacy Plan

Just as you have a plan for school improvement, you should have a plan for your advocacy efforts. Crafting an advocacy plan includes several distinct steps. Designing an Advocacy Plan summarizes the steps. First and foremost is to be clear about the issue. Be as specific as you can about what you want to achieve. For example, your focus may be increasing content literacy in classrooms at your school.

Then you need to identify goals and accompanying strategies, learn about your allies and opponents and those who might emerge as allies or opponents, and develop advocacy strategies and identify opportunities to impact their thinking. Finally, you need to implement your plan and monitor its results.

Designing an Advocacy Plan

Step 1: Identify the issue.
Step 2: Be clear about your goals and accompanying strategies.
Step 3: Identify strengths and weaknesses of your current status.
Step 4: Develop two lists of goals and strategies: those for accomplishing future plans and one for promoting existing initiatives. Note which strategies will be effective with allies, and which ones are needed for potential opponents.
Step 5: Implement strategies.
Step 6: Monitor plans and assess results.
Step 7: Adjust plan as needed.

A more detailed discussion about planning, implementing, and sustaining a plan to achieve your school's vision is included in Chapter 3.

Be Clear About Stakeholders

Every school community has both internal and external stakeholders, people who have a "stake" in the success of your school. It's easy to focus on the groups inside your school, but groups outside the school also have a "stake" in your success. They often shape public opinion and influence decision makers.

Examples of Stakeholder Groups

Internal	External
• Teachers; • Other staff; • Students; • Administrative team; • School volunteers.	• Families; • School board; • Business leaders; • Senior citizens; • Neighbors without children in the school; • Media.

We'd encourage you to use the Stakeholders in Your School tool to think about your own school community and identify the specific stakeholder groups.

Stakeholders in Your School

Stakeholder Groups	
Internal	External

Each group will have differing needs for information and you may need to develop a diverse set of strategies to inform them of your work and engage them as partners in your school improvement efforts.

Internal Stakeholders

In Chapter 3 we talked about ways to involve and inform stakeholders, including internal groups. First, it is important to recognize that everyone who works or attends your school may not have the same level of support for your vision and improvement plans. Second, regardless of the level of support, it's critical to develop a plan to work with staff members to nurture and sustain momentum toward your shared vision.

Consider your own setting and your internal stakeholders. This chart can help you think about what you're currently doing and additional things you might consider.

Working With Internal Stakeholders

	Current Strategies	**Things to Consider**
Create opportunities for teachers and other staff to be involved in planning for our school's initiatives.		
Provide multiple forms of professional development to help increase capacity for our school's initiatives.		
Communicate in a variety of ways.		
Engage both supporters and detractors in conversations about our school's initiatives and strategies for our school's initiatives.		
Attend to your own professional growth and development about your school's initiatives.		
Model the use of the initiatives in your daily interactions with staff.		

Advocacy ◆ 83

	Current Strategies	Things to Consider
Share examples of best practices from within your school and from other sites.		
Understand that not everyone will embrace your vision.		

External Stakeholders

Schools do not exist in isolation. They are part of the fabric of every community and reflect community values and priorities. The external community, like your internal community, is comprised of groups with very different needs for information and access to the school. Examples of external stakeholders include families, the school board, the business community, senior citizens, neighbors of the school, and the media.

Movers and Shakers

In very community there are individuals known as "movers and shakers." They are people who are recognized leaders in their area, formal or informal, and who others turn to for guidance on important issues. Each is someone who is able to get things done by rallying support, identifying resources, and building coalitions.

Characteristics of "Movers and Shakers"

- Articulate spokespersons;
- Respected for their knowledge;
- Able to convince others of their point of view;
- Skilled at identifying and securing resources;
- Connected to other "movers and shakers";
- Powerful and influential;
- Often energetic and initiate change;
- Seen as able to influence the future.

Think about your own school. Who would you place on your list of "movers and shakers"? You may list a parent, but there might also be a "mover and shaker" who doesn't have children in your school. Also describe why you included each person on your list. Move throughout the tool to consider your school district. Who are the "movers and shakers" in your district? What characteristics do they possess? Finally, consider people outside your immediate area. Frequently, the most influential "movers and shakers" are outside of your school or district. They may be influential politicians, policy makers, or community development personnel.

Movers and Shakers

Movers and Shakers in Your School	
Names	Characteristics
1.	1.
2.	2.
3.	3.
4.	4.
Movers and Shakers in Your District and/or Community	
Names	Characteristics
1.	1.
2.	2.
3.	3.
4.	4.
Movers and Shakers Beyond Your School, District, and/or Community	
Names	Characteristics
1.	1.
2.	2.
3.	3.
4.	4.

Advocacy Tools

Successful advocacy is more than just having passion for your school and its future. It requires that you develop, and use, a set of strategies to share your message and mobilize others to support your vision.

Build a Network

To be truly effective, you need to build a network of people who can help with your efforts. Remember, communication is a two-way street, so this group will serve two purposes: to help you understand how stakeholders in various groups perceive a situation and to help you communicate your message.

One model is the Key Communicator Network, developed by the National School Public Relations Association. It includes a series of steps that help you identify key people to invite to participate and ideas for how you can work with them to advocate for your vision.

Building a Key Communicator Network

1. Bring together a small group of trusted people who know the community. Brainstorm with those whom others listen to. While the bank president may be an opinion leader, so might the barber, cab driver, bartender, or supermarket checkout clerk.
2. Create a workable list from all the names that have been gathered to invite to join your network. Make sure that all segments of the community are represented.
3. Send a letter to the potential members, explaining that you want to create a new communications group for your school to help the community understand the challenges, successes, and activities of your school. In the letter, invite the potential members to an initial meeting and include a response form.
4. Make follow-up phone calls to those who do not return the response form, especially those who will be most important to have on your network.
5. Start the initial meeting by explaining that those in the audience have been invited because you see them as respected community members who care about the education students are being provided. Also, point out that you believe schools operate best when the community understands what is taking place and becomes involved in providing the best possible learning opportunities for students.

Then, describe the objectives of a Key Communicator Network:

- To provide network members with honest, objective, consistent information about the school;
- To have the network members deliver this information to others in the community when they are asked questions or in other opportunities; and
- To keep their ears open for any questions or concerns community members might have about the school. Those concerns should be reported to the principal or person in charge of the network so communication efforts can deal with those concerns. (It's always best to learn about concerns when one or two people have them instead of when 20 or 30 are vocally sharing them with others.)

Ask the invitees for a commitment to serve on the network and find out the best way to communicate with them, i.e. e-mail, fax, or telephone.

6. Establish a Key Communicator Network newsletter specifically for these people. After the first year, send out a short evaluation form to see how the network is working and might be improved.

For more information about Key Communicator Networks, contact the National School Public Relations Association, 301.519.0496 and purchase a copy of *A Guidebook for Opinion Leader/Key Communicator Programs*.

Consider your own school community. How would you build a Key Communicator Network? Who might be involved? How would you get started?

Creating Your Key Communicator Network

1. Who would you bring together to talk about building a network? Who would you talk with about the group? How would you assure all segments of your community are represented?	
2. How will you extend an invitation to potential members and explain the purpose of the group? How will you create a sense of urgency and importance for their participation?	
3. How do you plan to organize the initial meeting? Where will the meeting be held? How will you share your vision? How will you listen and gather feedback from members?	

4. What process will you use to both gather and share information with the network? How will you keep members engaged in the work?

The One-Page Fact Sheet

A "One Page Fact Sheet" helps you organize the important facts and points of your issue. It can be used as a handout to be shared with others and it will give you necessary background information, as well as added confidence to discuss your issue. One page is your limit. Most decision makers want the basic facts and don't want wasted time. The limit also enables you to keep your message focused.

Key Points in a One-Page Fact Sheet

Clearly define the issue.
State your position on the issue.
Clarify what you want the decision maker to do. Define five talking points in order of importance. Provide two references to support issue.
Make the sale with a closure statement.

Elevator Talk

There are times when you only have a brief opportunity to make personal contact with a key decision maker. As the old adage says, you only have one chance to make a first impression. In those cases, you should be prepared to give a personal story about the importance of your issue. Elevator talks should only be for a one- or two-story building—the time it takes an elevator to travel one or two floors—and no more than 30 seconds. People tire quickly of tedious talk about an issue, particularly when part of a casual encounter.

Elements of an Elevator Talk

1. Your name and what you do;
2. Your key issue;
3. What you would like the person to know.

Work with another person to practice telling your story and why you care about this issue. When you first share your story it may feel stilted and formal. With practice it becomes more natural and informal. Practice will give you confidence when you have a chance or planned meeting with a stakeholder or "mover and shaker." Having an effective "elevator talk" is essential in networking, engaging partners, and opening new doors. First impressions are easily sabotaged with an elevator talk that's unimpressive because it's too long or too short.

Advocacy With Your School Board

School boards set district policy and determine the allocation of funds. Board members are often community leaders who have influence with other members of the community. By gathering support from the school board you can build momentum for your improvement plans through the networks and alliance of board members.

Your school board is different from any other stakeholder group. Because they set policy and allocate resources, it is important to always connect your vision for your school with the board's vision for the district.

There are some other steps that we've found to be really important when interacting with your school board. After reviewing the suggestions, you can use the strategies below to create a plan.

Strategies for Interacting With Your School Board

- Identify a parent or community spokesperson to help deliver your message to the board.
- Frame the importance of your plans in your opening statement. Link it to board goals and how students will be successful once they leave your school.
- Describe your plan in such a way that the board can see the link between your overall school improvement efforts and their goals.
- Share examples of your work to illustrate the impact. It can be very helpful to highlight the effect of your plans on one or more students.
- Give recognition to the individuals who have contributed to your success. It is a time for you to be modest and allow others to be recognized.
- Conclude your presentation by aligning your school's vision with the board's vision for the district.

Advocacy With Parents and Families

Parents and families are important allies in improving your school's program. Not only do they support your efforts with their children, they can be advocates for your school with their friends, extended family, and connections throughout the community.

We suggest three strategies for your advocacy work with families. First, communicate often and with lots of information. Second, provide meaningful roles for parents in school life so that they can see your work to improve your school. Third, provide support and resources so that they can be successful with their children at home. Using the tool below, consider the three strategies, your current efforts in that area, and other options you might implement.

Parent and Family Advocacy Tools

Strategy	How We Do This Now	What We Need to Consider
Communication Strategies (include a variety of media including print and electronic)		
Provide Meaningful Involvement (provide ways for families to be involved beyond traditional PTO and bake sales)		

Strategy	How We Do This Now	What We Need to Consider
Provide Support and Resources (identify information and resources needed to work with their children)		

Advocacy and Emerging Technology

Technology is a powerful advocacy tool. As the president has recently demonstrated, Twitter and other forms of social media can engage constituents, provide information, and shape public opinion. Like it or not, technology is part of the everyday fabric of American life.

We've found that there are several technology tools to include in your advocacy initiatives. They include your school's website, blogs, and social media accounts like Facebook, Twitter, Instagram, and YouTube.

The dilemma with technology is that it is constantly changing. Social media tools that are popular become unpopular. People become reluctant to use social media because of concerns about privacy. Or a new and better social media tool emerges.

Your School Website

Your school's website is often the first place families go for information about your school. People expect the site to provide basic information about the school, its programs and activities, and contact information.

While most school websites are governed by district policy and fit a unique format, many districts provide a link to each school's unique web page. Here are some tips about how to assure that people return again and again (Williamson & Johnston, 2012):

Keep It Fresh and Original—One of the most important things about a web presence is the need to keep it original and fresh. Updated content is absolutely critical. People visit sites to gather information and the presence of fresh, original content will bring them back again and again.

Know Your Audience—A good website recognizes the audience that will be using it and provides content that is relevant to the audience. Choose headlines and text that align with your audience's needs. Remember your audience and use a human voice when writing content. A conversational tone is better received than one that uses educational jargon and a formal tone.

Make It Easy to Navigate—A good website has content that is easy to locate and use. Name pages and links so that people will easily understand. Routinely check to see that links are working and make sure most content is no more than a single click away from the homepage. If there is a lot of content, include a search box so that visitors can easily find what they are looking for.

Clean, Simple, Professional Design—Pay attention to the look of your site. Be sure colors contrast well and the font of your text makes reading easy. Remember that lots of text can make locating information difficult. Use sub-headings or bullet points to improve the layout.

Expand the Content Through Links—Include links that will take users to additional content. For example, you might link to a parent resource center or information on college admissions that makes your site the "one stop parent resource" on school related issues. Providing unique and interesting content is a sure way to get families and community to return to your site again and again.

Blogs

You've probably read a blog on some of the websites you've visited. A blog is basically a website that functions like an online journal or personal diary. The power of a blog is that you can make it whatever you want it to be. It is a website where you write content, can link to other sites and information, and can invite people to comment on your entries or e-mail you about your entry.

Many principals and other school leaders use a blog as one way to share their thoughts about school programs, activities, and issues. It can be a useful way to share your school's successes and to share the good work of your teachers and students.

Basically, a blog is "good" if it attracts viewers and they choose to return. But generally there are three criteria that define the functioning of an effective blog.

- **Frequency**—The most effective blogs include frequent postings that are compelling enough to attract readers to return to see what you are thinking and writing about.
- **Brevity**—Blogs are best characterized by relatively brief postings on a topic that may include links to other resources or information.
- **Personality**—Blogs are generally written in the first person and build a social link to readers by reflecting the writer's individual point of view. The blog is almost like a good friend, one you trust and one who may help you solve problems (Rettburg, 2008).

Social Media

Social media can help create a community where your students, teachers, families, and community can gather and share information, interact, and build your school's image and reputation.

Increasingly families and community turn to online resources, like Facebook and Twitter, as a way to learn about schools and other educational organizations, to identify their strengths and challenges, and to assist in making decisions about school programs and placement.

A principal in Mukilteo, Washington told us about his experience with social media. For many of the families at his school their smart phone is the primary means of communication. They don't have a landline and they often have limited Internet connections in their home. But they do have a phone that connects to the Internet. So, the school uses Twitter to share information about Open House and parent meetings, or to spread the word about school closings. As he said, "It's just another tool that helps us stay in touch with our families."

Having a presence on Facebook, Twitter, Instagram, or other social media sites helps to establish your school as one that is comfortable with a more transparent presence and allows you to more quickly disseminate information about your school. When you create a social media presence, always build a link to your school's accounts from your school website.

Every year we find more schools using social media to share information about their programs, their students, and to engage families and community in school life. Here are some of the ways social media may be used in your school.

- Share photos and brief biographies of new teachers;
- Post news about your sports teams and game results;
- Share the daily lunch menu;
- Provide information about school closings;
- Announce meetings and events;
- Share links to educational news and articles about your school;
- Post short videos from school concerts or dramatic presentations;
- Announce opportunities to volunteer at your school.

Plan for Use of Emerging Technologies

Form of Technology	Goals	Action Items
Website		
Blogs		

Form of Technology	Goals	Action Items
Social Media		

Advocacy and the Media

At some point, you will likely be required to deal with the media, whether it is your local newspaper or some form of electronic media. Don't be taken by surprise; anticipate that you will need to communicate with the media and plan appropriately. Preparation is your friend. You might keep our tips for Dealing With the Media available as a reminder of ways you can be an effective advocate with the media.

Dealing With the Media

- Preparation is your best friend. Learn as much as you can about the reporter, the show, and the audience.
- Establish your communication goals for each interview.
- Determine two or three key points to make to reach your goal.
- Speak in "memorable language."
- Learn and use the "bridging technique." Redirect the interview to your key points.
- Practice, practice, practice. Practice on camera if possible.
- Do not wear clothes or use mannerisms that distract from your message.
- Forget jargon, now and forever.
- Make sure that the mind is in gear before the mouth travels.
- Look at the reporter when answering questions; turn to the camera when delivering a key point.
- Steady eyes suggest honesty; blinking, darting eyes suggest nervousness and dishonesty.
- Anticipate questions and have answers ready. Once the interview is scheduled, try to figure out what questions the reporter might ask.
- Relax.

Advocacy in an Era of School Choice

One specific challenge for today's school leaders is advocating for his or her school when parents have choices as to where their kids attend school. Depending on your state, students may attend traditional public schools, charter schools, private schools, or online schools. How do you advocate for the positive aspects of your school, moving beyond test scores? The suggestions we've previously discussed can be effective, but you will find additional suggestions below.

Tips for Helping Your School Stand Out Among Other Options

- Build a consistent, appealing brand, image, and design. If needed, bring in a consultant for advice.
- Create a student marketing club for help.
- Gain information about families moving to the area or students who are not currently attending your school from realtors, the Chamber of Commerce, or feeder schools if appropriate.
- Have general message materials, but also provide specific information focused on particular audiences, such as new parents, realtors, and parents of multiple kids.
- Address critical issues parents care about.
- Be sure all your materials leverage your online presence. Put your web address and social media information on letterhead, envelopes, and signage.
- Be sure your website is easy to navigate and runs at an appropriate speed. People become frustrated when it is hard to find information, when it takes too many clicks to get to key information, and it is too slow.
- Increase the visibility of your web presence using keywords that are used in searches (such as "best school in <your city>") or through a tool such as Google Adwords.
- Create a school blog, which includes written information and videos. Include posts from students, teachers, and parents.

Advocacy Scorecard

Barbara's father is a successful advocate in North Carolina where he provides information about the importance of healthy lifestyles for children and adolescents. He shared with us a strategy for assessing the status of your advocacy efforts. We've adapted his work into an Advocacy Scorecard below, which principals can use to measure their advocacy work (Blackburn, Blackburn, & Williamson, 2018).

Advocacy Scorecard

Directions: Score your advocacy work by awarding 1–10 points for each of the following items.

_____ 1. My school has a written plan to partner with others.

_____ 2. We are open to building partnerships with other schools and groups.

_____ 3. We build links to websites as a way to assist our partners.

_____ 4. We know how to communicate effectively with other groups.

_____ 5. We understand the human relations skills necessary for our partners to work successfully together.

_____ 6. We understand the cultures that every school and organization brings to our partnership work.

_____ 7. We enjoy sharing successes with our partners.

_____ 8. There is regular, routine communication among our local, district, and state partners.

_____ 9. We understand the pitfalls of working with partners and have developed strategies for avoiding them.

_____ 10. We partner with other schools and with agencies in education and related fields in support of our school's vision.

0–20	Do you really want to be an advocate?
21–40	It's time to think about what you do.
41–60	You have a solid foundation for advocacy.
61–80	You know the meaning of empowerment.
81–100	You have an excellent plan for advocacy.

How did you do? Where are your strengths as an advocate and where are opportunities for growth?

Final Thoughts

As a school leader, you find yourself advocating for your school. You talk with teachers and other staff. You talk with families. You build networks with community groups inside and outside of education and you interact with people in the central office. It is important for leaders to recognize this important role and strengthen their skills to hone a clear message about the importance of their school improvement efforts.

Where Do I Begin?

If...	Then...
You would like to see if you are ready to be an advocate,	Reflect using the self-assessment.
You'd like to identify who can help you in your advocacy efforts,	Check out the sections on internal and external stakeholders and movers and shakers.
You need to know what to do once you identify stakeholders and who might participate in advocacy efforts,	Review the Key Communicator Network ideas.
You need suggestions for sharing information and gaining support for your school,	Look at the sections on advocating to families, using technology, and promoting you school in an era of choice.

7

Shared Accountability

One of the biggest roadblocks to change in schools is the resistance from teachers, students, parents, and other building and district leaders. As we discussed earlier, every person deals differently with change. Some are more accepting, others more resistant.

No change initiative is successful unless shared accountability is a part of the process. We suggest that teachers, families, and students as well as school and district leadership have a role in accountability.

Accountability is much more than issuing mandates and expecting compliance. For school leaders it involves energizing and motivating individuals and groups.

The culture of the school must be one where high value is placed on improving students' educational experience, where there is a collective commitment to improvement and a parallel commitment to supporting people who take risks and make changes. Further, the culture must not accept failure as an option. Every student must be expected to learn and the staff must be committed to supporting students in their learning.

Families and community are also integral to school success. School personnel must work with families and community members to ensure that students have the resources to be successful in school and families must be engaged in school life through participation in school governance and responsibility for student success.

Supporting Teachers and Other Staff

Part of the resistance to change is driven by the expectation that people will be held accountable for results. Successful leaders understand that the success of any change initiative is directly related to developing the capacity of the people in the organization to implement the change. The *School Administrators of Iowa*, a professional organization for principals, identified several research-based strategies that principals can use to support people during change (Gold & Roth, 1999). They include the following practices.

Ways to Support Teachers and Staff During Change

- Allow people to discuss feelings of loss and the difficulty of "letting go" of familiar programs and practices;
- Identify the needs of individual people and tailor the support based upon need;
- Develop support groups that are problem solving, action oriented, and non-judgmental;
- Be candid about unmet needs and work with people to plan specific ways to meet the need;
- Focus on strengths, skills, and interests of each person;
- Provide opportunity for everyone involved to share their ideas and talents;
- Plan ways for individuals to expand their skills to support the innovation;
- Develop personal development plans tailored to each individual involved in implementing the innovation;
- Identify ways that individuals can work to support one another throughout the implementation;
- Focus on successes and achievements;
- Give extra support to those who need it;
- Keep communication open and encouraging.

Source: Adapted from Gold and Roth (1999)

Overcoming Resistance

People respond to change in different ways. Some (5%) are early adopters and eagerly embrace any innovation. Another 5% will never adopt a change; nothing can get them to embrace the innovation. But most people (90%) can be moved toward support if given sufficient time and information.

We've found that people resist change for two primary reasons. They don't see the value of the change or they are not sure they will be as successful with the change. We've found this to be true when working with teachers and principals on all sorts of projects like differentiating instruction, or even changing school organization and structure.

Some of the most frequent concerns involve changing long-standing practices like grading or classroom organization. We often find intense resistance to the idea of a "Not Yet" grading policy. Teachers may find it cumbersome to implement. Parents may say it doesn't hold students accountable. School leaders may not know how to explain it to parents and community members.

Maslow's hierarchy (1968) is a useful way to think about what happens to people when asked to change. Under stress people may move to a lower level on the hierarchy. With support they are able to move to higher levels.

Example of Staff Needs	
Aesthetic Need (self-actualization)	Focus on the needs of students first.
Need for Understanding Need for Knowledge	What do I need to know to be successful? What opportunities will I have for professional growth? What models exist that can help me plan for the change?
Esteem Needs Belonging Needs	Will I be successful changing my instruction? Will others (colleagues, students, parents) value my work? How do the new norms around align with my beliefs?
Security Needs Survival Needs	What will I be teaching? Will I be successful in this new design? Will I have sufficient materials to provide a rich experience for students? Do I have the knowledge and skills for success? Who's making these decisions?

Source: Adapted from Maslow (1968); Williamson & Blackburn (2016)

It's not just teachers who deal with the complexities of change. It also affects students, families, and leaders.

Examples of Other Stakeholders' Needs			
	Students	**Families**	**Leaders**
Aesthetic (self-actualization)	Focus on own learning first	First priority is supporting child's success	Every action supports success for every student
Need for Understanding *Need for Knowledge*	Will I have the knowledge to be successful? What level of support will I have?	Do I have the information to support my child's success? What examples are available to help me support my child?	Do I have the knowledge and skills to work with teachers, students, and families to make this change?
Esteem Needs *Belonging Needs*	Will I be successful? What will others think of me if I work hard?	Will I be successful changing family habits about this change?	What will other school leaders think of my work on this effort?
Security Needs *Survival Needs*	What happens if I am unsuccessful? Do I have the knowledge and skills for success?	What happens if my child and I disagree about the importance of school work?	Will my school be successful? Do I have the knowledge and skills to sustain our efforts to implement this change?

Source: Adapted from Maslow (1968); Williamson & Blackburn (2016)

Collaboration Connection

Choose the stakeholders you anticipate being resistant to change, whether it is a parent or business partner. Use the information about Maslow to have a conversation with them about their concern.

Have a Clear, Concrete Result

One way to help overcome resistance is to have a clear, concrete result. Teachers and families often need to see a clear, defined outcome. You should always be able to describe what success looks like. For example, "If we are successful implementing _____, we will know it because we will see _____."

You do not need to develop the vision without any input; the most successful, and lasting, visions are shared ones. However, when working to implement a specific change, you should be able to provide an explicit, measurable result.

Examples of Clear, Concrete Results

- Teachers will use more analysis and synthesis questions with students;
- Students will be able to describe ways that they are supported in their work;
- Students, teachers, and families can discuss ways that student work samples have changed; and
- Teachers can explain how classroom routines have been modified to provide time for students to revise and resubmit work.

Building Accountability Into Everyday Routines

The most important role of a school leader is supervising the instructional program. But the principal is not the only person responsible for a quality instructional program. Teachers and other staff are responsible for delivering instruction and positively impacting every student's learning.

Principals are, however, responsible for creating a climate and culture at their school that supports quality instruction, promotes innovation, and nurtures professional growth.

Ways to Focus Your Culture

- Creating a structure that provides time for collegial discussion and dialogue about the proposed change;
- Staying current on educational trends and developments;
- Accessing professional development and other resources to your proposed change;
- Modeling good instructional practices at meetings and during other interaction with staff; and
- Attending and actively participating in professional development and other learning opportunities about the proposed change.

Accountability Through Supervisory Practices

Through the supervisory process principals can raise the level of accountability. Glickman et al. (2018) suggest that effective supervision is an ongoing process. It is much more than just evaluating teacher performance. It is all about engaging teachers in reflective conversations about their practice. Effective supervisors understand that teachers are adults and respond well to the principles of adult learning. Effective supervisors are empowering and motivating and provide opportunities for teachers to reflect on and think about their teaching.

Two examples illustrate the importance of these activities. At Crossroads High School in Georgia the principal and others conduct weekly instructional walkthroughs. While not unusual, at Crossroads they identify a specific instructional emphasis. If that emphasis is not observed, at the end of the third walkthrough the principal schedules a time to talk with the teacher and identify steps to incorporate the practice into instruction.

We've developed an example of a walkthrough. This specific protocol can be used to focus on indicators but you can develop a protocol that addresses your school improvement priorities. A portion of the protocol is provided here.

Rigorous Schools and Classrooms Walkthrough

This protocol is used to gather data about the school's progress implementing the rigorous schools and classrooms indicators. It is not designed to be part of personnel evaluation. The protocol is useful in identifying school-wide trends and issues.

Indicator	Notes and Questions
Learner-Centered Instruction • Teachers maintain high expectations for all students. • Support and scaffolding are provided to ensure success. • There is evidence of student high-order thinking. • Students are active in all aspects of learning. • Lessons incorporate application activities seamlessly.	*Expectations for Learning* • Teachers are consistent in the belief that students can learn, will learn, and that they have the power to help them do so. • Lessons are designed so students see the value of specific learning. • Teachers are persistent in supporting student learning. • Interaction with students reflects the belief that it is unacceptable to not learn.

The principal of Chapin Middle School in Chapin, South Carolina uses a weekly newsletter to highlight information about their school goals and examples that have been observed throughout the school.

In *The Principalship from A to Z* (2016) we describe a model for effective supervision. Centered on improving teacher instruction, it includes a pre-conference and a post-observation conference. We've found that the best instructional conferences provide ample opportunity for the teacher to process and reflect on his or her own practice.

Almost all school districts have an established evaluation process including established timelines and forms. Often those processes don't include time for the teacher to reflect on their practice and to identify strategies to strengthen and enhance their instruction.

We recognize the legal requirements that school leaders must follow but we also suggest a process that provides for ample discussion of both before and following an observation.

Some of the most productive conversations occur following the classroom observation. Teachers value the time to think about their work and reflect on its success.

The process of reflection is a critical part of implementing an instructional innovation. Often the most skilled teachers are most interested in an opportunity to reflect on their teaching and consider ways to grow professionally.

The most useful prompts are open-ended. They do not lend themselves to a single answer and are designed to promote teacher reflection. The discussion cannot be seen as evaluative nor punitive. It must be supportive and encourage professional growth.

Suggested Post-Observation Discussion Prompts

- Thank you for the opportunity to visit your classroom. I would like to have you talk with me about the lesson.
- When you plan a lesson, what things do you consider? How do you plan to address our goal of _____ for students?
- Describe ways that you monitor student learning during your lessons? What clues do you gather about student learning?
- As you continue to implement _____, what do you consider the appropriate next steps?
- What additional support or resources may I provide for you? How can I support your effort to implement _____ in your classroom?

Accountability Through Professional Development

Professional development is another essential tool for realizing your vision and supporting school improvement. As discussed in Chapter 4, you need to have a clear purpose linked to research and data about student needs.

You must also assure accountability for the use of professional development in classrooms. We believe that one of the most effective means to accountability is that of one person to another. At one school where Ron worked, teachers were responsible for sharing one new idea they implemented at the first staff meeting after any professional development activity. They met in small groups, shared their ideas, and asked for suggestions and feedback from colleagues. This shared accountability led to greater use of the innovations.

There are other ways that you can assure accountability for the use of professional development. They include an instructional walkthrough organized and led by teachers, an opportunity to examine student work samples or lesson study activities. You might also ask for samples of student work rather than request to see lesson plans.

Accountability Through School Improvement

Too often school improvement is not linked to the school's vision. It is driven by either local or state requirements to have a School Improvement Plan. We suggest that you use your school improvement process as a tool to support the shared vision you develop with teachers, families, and other stakeholders.

In one school district outside of Detroit, Ron led a project to improve the quality of the middle school program. After developing a shared vision for their school, the group examined data about student learning, student demographics, and teacher and student perceptions about the learning environment. These data then guided decisions about organizing the instructional day.

Most importantly, the group agreed on a set of indicators, or data points, that would be routinely monitored by the School Improvement Team in each school. They committed to using that data to guide decisions about both short-term and long-term school improvement goals.

Accountability Through Work With Families and Community

Families and community also have a role in accountability. In Chapter 6 we suggested that you develop a set of talking points that you can use to build support for your vision. It is also important to provide families with the information and tools they need to support your vision and the school's improvement initiatives.

We believe it is important to be proactive rather than reactive when talking with stakeholder groups. One principal in suburban Phoenix asked his staff to share "turnaround" stories with him—stories of students who made a significant positive change in their learning. He always had two or three different stories that he could share with families, in formal and informal conversation about the school.

When Barbara went to a curriculum night at Apple Valley Middle School in Fletcher, North Carolina, she immediately noticed the school's core belief—learning is not optional. That message was shared with families and reinforced throughout the evening's activities.

We've found that families are almost always supportive of increasing their child's school. Often, however, they want specific ideas about how they can be helpful. Here is a list of ideas we've learned from our work with teachers and principals.

Sample Ideas for Supporting Parents

- Provide tips for how to organize the home to support completing homework;
- Help families locate libraries and other helpful online resources;
- Organize parent support groups;
- Create a parent library with books and materials about parenting and children's academic growth;
- Include tips for parents in every school newsletter;
- Arrange for parents to share ideas and strategies for supporting their child's success in school.

These efforts help reinforce your vision and provide families and community with tangible results of your efforts.

Possible Talking Points

- Current data about student learning (assessments, major projects, and assignments);
- Awards and recognitions received by students and staff;
- Examples of students who made a positive change in their learning;
- Scholarships students earned;
- Teachers who did "whatever it takes" to ensure student success.

In Hall County, Georgia, there is a commitment to rigor for all students. The Hall County Schools have an Assistant Director of Teaching and Learning with responsibility for instruction.

We want to thank Dr. Sally Krisel, Director of Innovative and Advanced Programs, for allowing us to share a letter they use to let parents know about their work to improve rigor for all students.

Dear Parents,

On our web page, in other publications, and in our daily work here in Hall County Schools, we are focused on the motto **"Character, Competency, and Rigor ... for All."** But what do we mean by the term "rigor"?

Essentially, we believe that mastery of challenging and meaningful content must be our goal for *all* students. Whether they are performing at, below, or above the levels of their age peers, all students deserve an education that challenges them just above their current levels of development. I believe that every student should come to school every day thinking, *"Wow, this class is tough! But I know my teacher will help me, and I know that if I work hard, I can do it!"*

We must ask all students, including those who can quite easily achieve "adequate" indicators of achievement by No Child Left Behind (NCLB) standards, to stretch, to achieve at levels commensurate with their peers, not just nationally but internationally! There is great power in high expectations, and I believe that all our young people can do far more than we have typically asked them to do. Taking this proficiency view of students, i.e., focusing on their strengths and interests as we increase the level of academic challenge, is the best way to change the culture of schools. Simply put, adequacy is not enough for our children; we must have excellence!

I would also like to clarify what we believe rigor is NOT. It is not just asking our children to do more of the same (*"Complete all the problems on page 30 ... PLUS the bonus problems."*). Yes, we want our children to be engaged in curriculum that pushes them, but not in a joyless, repetitive sense. As I work with teachers on ways to raise the academic bar, we are also talking about ways to make curriculum more meaningful and interesting for students. In summary, we are asking teachers to improve the "authenticity" of the work they ask students to do. Using the language of Dr. Fred Newmann's *Authentic Intellectual Work*, we are focusing on the following:

- **Construction of Knowledge**—We want students to *use* what they learn, not just repeat it. Students should be asked to grapple with information and ideas by synthesizing, generalizing, explaining, and drawing conclusions that produce new understandings for them—just the things that we as adults do in the world of work!
- **Disciplined Inquiry**—Instruction must focus on important concepts within the discipline, and students should learn them with such thoroughness that they are capable of exploring connections and relationships so they have a deeper understanding of the subject. Also, students should be able to discuss subject matter in depth with their classmates and their teachers in ways that build improved understanding.

- **Value Beyond School**—Rigorous curriculum should have clear connections to students' lives. We want our teachers helping students see the connections between substantive knowledge and either public problems or personal experiences in their lives outside of school.

Commitment to rigorous curriculum means that we envision each learner on an "escalator of development" and envision ourselves—teachers and parents working together—as seeing to it that each escalator moves steadily upward in all those areas required for persistent intellectual, emotional, and moral growth in all students. Here on the Rigor web page, we put the spotlight on some of the best examples of rigorous learning opportunities . . . and the extraordinary way Hall County students are responding!

Dr. Sally Krisel
Director of Innovative and Advanced Programs

Reprinted with permission of the Hall County Schools.

Collaboration Connection

Use the ideas for supporting parents to include extended family members. Also provide similar ideas for business partners. You might also offer to provide information to media outlets, whether it is a weekly newspaper, blog, or neighborhood social media source.

Accountability for Students

Students also share accountability for their own learning. Too often students aren't considered when thinking about accountability.

We believe students must be actively involved in their own learning, by making decisions about their learning and by being responsible for asking questions, being clear about their work, and completing assignments.

Students must also know the expectations for their work. Some of their most frequent questions include: what are the grading standards? Where do I go for additional support? How do I locate examples of a high-quality assignment? Where may I locate resources to complete my work?

We also believe that students need to know about new programs and practices and how those programs will impact their learning. They must be provided the knowledge and skills to be successful as new programs are implemented.

> ### Ways to Support Student Accountability
>
> - Provide exemplars for all work and rubrics that students can use to assess their success in completing assignments;
> - Inform students of new or revised grading practices;
> - Provide opportunities for students to revise and resubmit work;
> - Include support and scaffolding in classroom instruction;
> - Include engaging instructional activities connected to real life;
> - Act consistently on the belief that each student can learn, will learn, and your power to help them do so;
> - Provide quality and timely feedback on student work.

We recently learned of a program at East Fairmont Junior High School in Fairmont, West Virginia. It is called "Failure Is Not an Option" and built on the belief that student behaviors will not change until adult behaviors change. Christine Miller, Principal, shared the details of their program. It is designed to help learners understand their responsibility to complete work in a timely manner. They accept no excuses about failure to complete. Teachers handle all missing assignments up to three. After that, the office is informed and the student must report to the office to complete their work and failure results in removal from the regular lunchroom. Parents then get informed of the failure.

The "Failure Is Not an Option" program is a good example of changing practices to let students know about the commitment to their learning and success.

A school district in the state of Washington recently changed the daily schedule in its middle schools. They moved from a traditional seven-period day to an extended block with three classes meeting daily. This change required professional development for teachers, it required conversations with parents about the new structure, and it meant that students needed to understand the new design, how instruction would be different, and how they might need to rethink how they completed assignments and homework.

Neither students nor families were resistant to the block schedule. But it was a dramatic change from past practice and meant that both groups needed to know how the new day worked, and the implications for learning.

Focus and Refocus the Conversation

It is very easy to become distracted by personal agendas. All too frequently we've heard issues portrayed as impacting students when in fact it was an issue affecting a teacher or group of teachers.

At a recent workshop about developing a remediation plan for at-risk students, two teachers began to argue about classroom space and their own scheduling needs. The two continued to bicker for some time until the principal reminded everyone that the purpose of the remediation classes was to positively affect student learning for their neediest students. By reframing the conversation, the group was able to move beyond the personal agenda.

It is important to always keep your vision about change and your school improvement goals at the forefront of any conversation. Pulling the conversation back to an agreed-upon vision is one way to refocus the conversation.

A strategy that Ron uses when he works with schools on planning projects is to begin every meeting with an opportunity to review their vision. He includes the vision in the PowerPoint he uses and makes it one of the first things each group does. Ron asks each group to "Take a minute and read the vision statement. Think about how that statement can guide our work today."

Leadership in Action

Dan Ingham, Principal of John Glenn High School in the Wayne-Westland (Michigan) Schools has worked with his staff to implement significant changes in their school. Dan developed a set of his "Ten Commitments" that would guide his work with his staff. We think they provide a model for how other leaders can focus their school improvement work.

The Ten Commitments

1. Remain Focused on Learning for All: Consistently model the passion and persistence of our primary purpose—to help all students learn at high levels.
2. Develop and Sustain the School Structure and Culture as a Professional Learning Community (PLC): A PLC is defined as educators working in effective, high-performing collaborative teams, working interdependently, focused on collective inquiry, action research, and data driven best practices to achieve better results for students.
3. Organize Into Collaborative Culture: School will function as collaborative teams of professionals who work together interdependently to develop common pacing, design common assessments, and achieve common goals for which members are mutually accountable.
4. Provide for Job-Embedded Professional Development and Adult Learning: Raise student achievement by embedding ongoing and continuous professional development in the routine work of every educator.
5. Empower and Support Teacher Leadership: Develop the capacity of teachers throughout the school to assume leadership roles and view

herself or himself as a learning leader of leaders. Tap into everyone's "islands of excellence."
6. Stay Fixated on the Evidence of Learning: Every educator and every team will be expected to use results to inform and impact their professional practice, guide the process of continuous improvement, and facilitate continuous adult and student learning.
7. Implement a Balance of Summative and Formative Assessments: Use a balanced variety of assessments as a powerful tool for improving the teaching and learning process.
8. Assure a Systematic Response When Students Don't Learn: Ensure students who are not learning receive extra time and support that is timely, directive, and systematic. Create a system of tiered interventions of increasing intensity for students who struggle.
9. Enrich and Extend Learning for Students Already Proficient: Challenge and stretch all students by raising the academic bar. Ensure students of all abilities have clear opportunities for extra time and support and all students will benefit.
10. Celebrate, Celebrate, Celebrate: Publicly celebrate all improvements in behavior and results that will nourish the change effort. Emotionally reward hard workers and build momentum. Win small. Win early. Win often.

Source: From Ingham (2008)

It Starts and Ends With Me

During the last decade there has been a significant shift in accountability in schools. School staff share a collective accountability for the success of their students and every individual shares a personal responsibility and accountability for doing whatever it takes to ensure student success.

Ultimately it all starts and ends with each individual's personal vision for their school or classroom, their commitment to making the changes that are proposed, and their willingness to take risks, support one another, work collaboratively, and abandon long-standing practices that are not successful.

Our individual commitment to be held accountable for the success of our schools, our classrooms, and our students is what will make the biggest difference for students.

Final Thoughts

Improving your school is a shared responsibility requiring shared accountability. It is important to support teachers and other staff when implementing new programs or policies, individually and as a group. The focus must remain on continuous improvement rather than merely complying with mandates.

Where Do I Begin?

If...	Then...
You are having problems getting stakeholders to support your school's initiatives,	Review the suggestions for overcoming resistance.
You are looking for a way to use your administrative team to hold teachers accountable for initiatives,	Look at the section on supervisory practices.
You want to broaden shared accountability,	Check out the sections on accountability with parent and students.

8

Structures to Support School Improvement

The way your school is organized can support or inhibit school improvement efforts. The term "structure" is often associated with the physical plant, or structure, of a building. But we'll use the term in a broader, and more expansive, way.

Throughout the chapter we will discuss structures that support teachers, students, families, and leaders as they work with their school. We will include ways to build and support a collaborative culture, ideas for organizing teachers and students for instruction, and suggest several different ways to provide time for collaboration.

Professional Learning Communities

Almost every school has a structure in place for involving teachers and other staff in school improvement activities. Often they're called a professional learning community (PLC) and the term is common in many schools. A PLC is one way to think about working collaboratively to improve your school and your classrooms. PLCs take many forms, and have different tasks, but are almost uniformly focused on improving student learning.

Chapter 5: Professional Development provides a detailed description of professional learning communities and the way they can accelerate school improvement.

Central to the vitality of a professional learning community is a value on collaborative activity and a recognition that teachers and other personnel must be provided with time to meet, talk about instruction in your school, and identify strategies for improving your school. The central focus is on continuous improvement with a results orientation. One principal described it as a "laser light focus on getting the desired results."

Focus of Successful Professional Learning Communities

- Continuous program improvement;
- Rigorous, relevant curriculum and instruction;
- Interdisciplinary teaching and instructional teams.

Source: Adapted from Oxley, Barton, & Klump (2006, p. 3)

Time for Collaboration

It is important that teachers have time to work with colleagues on professional tasks. This collaborative time is one of the catalysts for nurturing and sustaining change. Teachers value the opportunity to meet with grade or content peers to discuss successes, diagnose ways to improve, develop a repertoire of strategies that they can use in their own classrooms, and provide critical input to school improvement plans.

There are many different ways to provide collaborative time. They vary considerably depending on the grade level of the school.

Ways to Provide Collaborative Time	
Common Planning	When teachers share a common planning period, some of the time may be used for collaborative work.
Parallel Scheduling	When special teachers (physical education, music, art, etc.) are scheduled so that grade level or content area teachers have common planning.

Shared Classes	Teachers in more than one grade or team combine their students into a single large class for specific instruction and the other teachers can collaborate.
Faculty Meeting	Find other ways to communicate the routine items shared during faculty meetings and reallocate that time to collaborative activities.
Adjust Start or End of Day	Members of a team, grade, or entire school agree to start their workday early or extend their workday one day a week to gain collaborative time.
Late Start or Early Release	Adjust the start or end of the school day for students and use the time for collaborative activity.
Professional Development Days	Rather than traditional large group professional development use the time for teams of teachers to engage in collaborative work.

Source: Adapted from Williamson (2009); DuFour, DuFour, Eaker, & Many (2006)

Angela Evans, the Instructional Dean at Tulsa Technology Center shared how her school provides collaborative time. They developed a "released time" schedule that allows every teacher to work with other teachers on instructional issues. The deans organize the schedule to provide two days during the year for this important work.

Regardless of the way you provide time for collaboration, the most important thing is how the time is used. It is important that it is productive and supports your school's vision.

Sample Tasks

- Meet in vertical teams to work on articulation of the curriculum;
- Work with grade-level teachers to examine student work;
- Talk with the School Improvement Team about conducting walk-throughs focused on a specific instructional task;
- Conduct a book study on *7 Strategies for Improving Your School.*

Organizing to Provide Collaborative Time

One way to provide additional collaborative time is to change the daily schedule. There are many different ways to organize the schedule (Williamson, 2009) but some provide more opportunity for collaboration than others.

Here are some of the ways we've found most effective at providing time for teachers to collaborate. We've grouped them into elementary and secondary examples but many of the strategies work in both settings.

Elementary School Examples

Location of Classrooms

Most elementary schools are organized into self-contained classrooms, particularly in the early grades. A common way to promote collaboration is to locate all early elementary classes on the same floor or in the same wing. Similarly, all the later elementary classes can be located near one another. One principal we met said that it "allowed each wing to focus on the developmental issues with their students" and "promoted collaboration among grade-level teachers."

Other schools we've visited place a class or two from each grade in a wing of the building. This organization is designed to provide interaction among the grades and ease the grouping and regrouping for instruction.

Of course, just locating classrooms near one another does not guarantee collaboration. It just provides the opportunity to collaborate. The key is to use the structure to promote collaboration and to have teachers work together on school improvement tasks.

Scheduling Special Classes

One way to provide collaborative time for teachers is to schedule special classes such as music, art, and physical education so that teachers at a single grade or combination of grades have common planning.

Many elementary teachers want an extended block of time in the morning for literacy and mathematics instruction. Since all special classes cannot be scheduled in the afternoon, it is important to talk with your teachers about how you might arrange for collaborative time.

Parallel Schedule

Many elementary schools organize classrooms to provide greater content-specific instruction, particularly in the upper grades. At each grade level one or two teachers might specialize in math and science and one or two others specialize in reading, language arts, and social studies.

By organizing all the teachers at a grade level so that they have a similar schedule, including when students go to special classes, you create time each day when those teachers can meet and collaborate. This time can be used to discuss instruction, develop common assessments, look at student work, diagnose student learning needs, or provide input to school improvement.

	1	2	3	4	5
Teacher A	Reading/LA	Reading/LA	S P E C I A L S	Reading/LA	Reading/LA
Teacher B	Reading/LA	Reading/LA		Reading/LA	Reading/LA
Teacher C	Math/Sci	Math/Sci		Math/Sci	Math/Sci
Teacher D	Math/Sci	Math/Sci		Math/Sci	Math/Sci

Secondary School Examples

Teaming

Many middle schools and some high schools organize students and teachers into instructional teams. A team may consist of a group of teachers who share students and often have common planning time to meet and talk about curricular and instructional issues.

There's lots of evidence about the positive impact of teaming on student learning and school climate when teams meet and spend most of their common planning time working on ways to improve student learning. We've found that the most effective teams are committed to talking about their instruction, about ways to increase align the curriculum of their classrooms, and about ways to provide additional support for student learning. Like all teams, if collaborative time is spent on routine day-to-day tasks, or if the team doesn't meet, the benefits are negligible.

School-Within-a-School

One way to respond to the anonymity present in large schools is to organize into smaller units, often called houses or small schools-within-a-school. In such a model students and teachers often remain in the same unit for most of the day.

Teachers in a school-within-a-school model often have common planning and a time to work collaboratively on instructional improvement.

Organization of Curricular Departments

Another strategy for promoting collaboration among teachers is to group curricular departments together rather than maintaining a separate organization. At New Trier High School, Northfield Campus, outside of Chicago, Principal Jan Borga put math and science teachers together into the same department. They shared office space and were expected to work collaboratively on curriculum design, interdisciplinary links, and instructional improvement. Her goal was to ensure a more challenging academic experience for students, one that maximized support and opportunity for learning. A similar arrangement occurred in other curricular areas.

Common Planning for Content Teachers

Yet another way to promote collaboration is to arrange the schedule so that teachers of a single course, or combination of courses, share a planning period. Richard Barajas, principal of Milby High School in Houston, Texas, organized the schedule of his Algebra teachers this way.

With common planning the Algebra teachers were expected to meet with one of the school's curricular specialists to design common assessments. Teachers were expected to teach the curriculum, use the assessments, and be prepared to discuss student success with the assessments. The discussions focused on what teachers learned about "what worked and what didn't work" in their lessons. They provided an opportunity to work collaboratively to redesign lessons that were less effective than desired and to reinforce practices that contributed to student success.

Collaboration Connection

One school Barbara worked with found a unique way to provide time for teachers to work together. Collaborating with parents and local business partners, other adults offered to lead clubs around different interests ranging from business to art. Once a week, clubs met for 30 minutes, which allowed for a brief opportunity to plan together.

Your School's Schedule as a Tool for School Improvement

Managing the school's schedule can be one of the most complex and time-consuming tasks faced by school leaders. Often the focus is on the logistics of the schedule but we've found that the most successful schools see the schedule as a tool that can be used to positively impact their instructional program.

The schedule can provide time for teachers to work together on strategies for school improvement. They can create varied instructional designs, provide additional support for students, and offer more in-depth instruction.

What is critical is to recognize that the school's schedule isn't a static, fixed structure but can be designed to promote your vision and support your school improvement priorities. Your school's schedule is a powerful tool to provide teachers with the tools they need to implement your shared vision.

Principles About School Schedules

- Schedules reflect a school's values and priorities;
- The most effective schedules are anchored in a shared vision;
- A quality schedule emerges when teachers and administrators work together in establishing priorities and selecting a design;
- Without clear goals, the schedule is merely a plan for organizing teachers and students; when guided by goals, the schedule becomes a powerful tool to positively impact teaching and learning.

Source: From Williamson and Blackburn (2016)

The first step is to talk with key stakeholders about the schedule. A shared vision and clarity of purpose helps build support for any schedule, particularly when it is being changed. For example, you might want to talk with your School Improvement Team about the current schedule, its strengths and challenges, and how it can support your improvement plans.

Organize the conversation around a series of questions designed to promote thinking and generate ideas. The staff at Bay Village Middle School in northern Ohio worked with Ron on just this issue. They organized their thinking around these three questions:

- How do we allocate time to content areas based on student need?
- What are several ways that we can create longer instructional blocks and provide regular time for teachers to collaborate?
- How do we provide flexibility so that students who need extra time or support have that option?

While these three questions addressed the needs at Bay Village, you will want to identify the questions appropriate to your own school and its needs. Starting with questions serves to organize the thinking and keep the discussion focused.

Value collaboration. We've found that building support among those responsible for implementing any initiative is important. Talk openly about every option. Discuss advantages and disadvantages. Communicate with stakeholders and provide an opportunity for them to provide suggestions and input. Chapter 3: Ownership and Shared Vision offers suggestions for ways to promote collaboration. Chapter 6: Advocacy provides ideas about communicating with stakeholders.

Time as a Resource

There are many different kinds of schedules. All have advantages and disadvantages and reflect values about the use of time, opportunity for collaboration, and the importance of providing additional support for students.

If you think of a schedule as simply a way of organizing teachers and students, then it limits the approaches you may consider. We recognize that every school faces constraints on their schedule. Things like shared teachers, transportation schedules, or the length of the school day can inhibit creativity.

But too often schools fall into the trap of past practice. The schedule looks remarkably similar from year to year. We suggest that you give yourself permission to think about alternative ways to use time and to recognize that time is a valuable resource, one that can be used to support your vision and your school improvement efforts.

The literature identifies several scheduling approaches that can be used to positively impact your school. We want to be very clear, however. The schedule is just a tool that creates a structure to improve your school. The key is how the time is used. It cannot be used merely to increase coverage. Here are some questions you might want to use as you think about changing your schedule.

- How will it provide greater depth in the curriculum?
- How will it strengthen and enhance instruction?
- How will it increase the opportunities for support for students?

We suggest that the creative and flexible use of time should become the norm in schools. Just as schools have begun to use technology to improve instruction, they can also use flexibility in their school day to promote some of the same activities.

We've found four characteristics of schools that are committed to the flexible use of time (Williamson, 2009). First, those schools use a variety of organizational arrangements, not linked to a specific schedule, or to adoption of teaming. Rather, those schools recognize that the need for time and flexibility may vary across content areas, or across days. So, each day of the week may vary from other days. Some subjects may have longer class periods than others. But flexibility is present and visible in the way time is used.

Second, teachers in these schools are empowered to make decisions about the use of time. That means that if there is a long block of time for a class, the teacher makes decisions about the use of that time, or a group or team of teachers works collaboratively to decide how time is used.

Third, there is a premium on flexibility and responsiveness in the routines of school life. Daily routines like taking attendance, scheduling lunch, visiting the media center, or walking to another part of the building aren't limitations. Rather, those routines adapt to meet the instructional needs of teachers and students.

Finally, we find that schools that value time as a resource are places where curricular and instructional practices are modified and take advantage of the flexibility in the schedule. Teachers value the opportunity to work with one another. Students value longer classes where there is a vibrant mix of direct instruction and application of their learning, and classes where assessment includes application of learning rather than memorization and repetition of facts.

Block Schedule

Block schedules provide long instructional blocks that teachers can use for greater instructional flexibility. Block schedules often release energy and creativity among teachers when they know they are not bound by a fixed period schedule.

Examples of activities possible with a longer block include regrouping for large- or small-group instruction; laboratory-type activities; team meetings; interdisciplinary or thematic units; learning activities that involve creating, building, or making a product; or additional support for student learning.

	Fixed Period Schedule	**Block Schedule**
1	Mathematics	Team decides on time given to each content area
2	Science	
3	Language Arts	
4	Social Studies	
5	Elective/Exploratory	Elective/Exploratory
6	Elective/Exploratory	Elective/Exploratory

Many middle and high schools have adopted a version of the block schedule commonly called a four-by-four block. In such a schedule each class is longer and fewer classes meet each day. At some schools the classes alternate from day to day. At others the classes meet daily and change at the end of the semester.

	Semester 1	**Semester 2**
1	Geometry	Concert Band
2	English 10	World History
3	Economics	Spanish 2
4	Physical Education	Biology

The four-by-four block schedule allows teachers to design lessons with opportunity for more in-depth instruction, time for guided practice, and more time to monitor student learning.

There are almost an infinite number of variations on the block schedule. For example, some schools use a four-by four block but longer blocks meet a few days each week, rather than every day. In Bothell, Washington the middle schools use a block schedule for six classes. Three classes meet on Monday and Thursday, four on Tuesday and Friday. Every class meets on Wednesday.

Other schools reverse the pattern and every class meets Monday, Wednesday, and Friday. Longer blocks are present on Tuesday and Thursday.

In each case, the design was purposeful and done to support the school's vision and its school improvement efforts.

Alternating Day Schedule

An additional scheduling tool is to alternate classes so that they do not meet every day. Alternating schedules may provide longer blocks of time for classes and are often used to provide an opportunity for students to take additional classes. Some schools use the alternating day schedule as a way to provide time for additional instruction or other support for students. Below is an example of an alternating schedule.

Mon	Tue	Wed	Thu	Fri
English	Spanish	English	Spanish	English
Math	Chemistry	Math	Chemistry	Math
Phys Ed.	US History	Phys Ed.	US History	Phys Ed.
Band	Drama	Band	Drama	Band

This example shows the schedule for one week. The next week the schedule would be reversed with the four classes meeting on Tuesday and Thursday meeting on Monday, Wednesday, and Friday.

Another example of an alternating day schedule builds in an every other day student support period. This support period is scheduled at the same time for every student. Students have time to access the testing center, meet with their counselor, work on longer assignments, meet with teachers, or conduct research for completing assignments.

Mon	Tue	Wed	Thu	Fri
Geometry	Orchestra	Geometry	Spanish	Geometry
French	Economics	French	Economics	French
Biology	**Support**	Biology	**Support**	Biology
Phys Ed.	English	Phys Ed.	Drama	Phys Ed.

Trimester Schedule

Yet another approach to organizing the school day is to use a trimester model. The school year is divided into three equal parts, with courses scheduled accordingly.

The ability for a student who fails a class to "recover" more quickly is one of the major advantages of a trimester model. In a traditional schedule a student might need to wait a full year before being able to retake a class. With the trimester model the student can repeat the class more quickly, the next trimester.

Some classes may meet one trimester, some two, and some even all three trimesters. Generally each class period is longer than in a traditional schedule and most classes meet only one trimester.

	Fall	Winter	Spring
1	Algebra 1	Biology	English 1B
2	English 1A	US History	Spanish 1B
3	Phys Ed.	Spanish 1A	Spanish 1B
4	Band	Band	Band

Regularities of the School Day

Every school has a set of routines that define the day. That can include passing time, arrival and departure, lunch, or before- and after-school activities. They are often just accepted as "the way things are around here" and not seen as a manifestation of the school's vision and culture.

We recognize the legal requirements for things like attendance and we understand the need to monitor student behavior and assure the safety of students and employees. But even while attending to those things, some schools have begun to rethink how they handle the "regularities" of the school day.

One high school in Oregon was concerned about the number of students who arrived early, or hung around at the end of the day. So, they did something rather novel. They held a series of informal conversations with the students in order to learn what was happening. They discovered that many of these students found school to be "one of the safest" places to be. They relied on the breakfast and lunch program, and there were few attractive options at home.

Rather than enforce the existing policies on arrival and departure, the school worked with religious and community groups to provide a comfortable, safe place for students to "hang out" before and after the school day. They created a student lounge with comfortable furniture, access to computers and other media, and staffed by community volunteers. The lounge is open from 7am until 6pm and has become a popular spot for students to gather. Some teachers and staff have begun to meet there with individuals or small groups and provide additional academic support.

Recently, several schools we've worked with have invested in creating coffee bars or coffee-free and specialty beverage carts available to students and staff. These carts capitalize on the popularity of coffee and tea products available nationwide. The difference is that they are run by student baristas under the direction of a faculty sponsor. In some schools, students who have a free period are allowed to patronize the coffee shop and talk with friends; in others the venue is only open during specific hours before or after school. Some even sell pastries and other things prepared in the cafeteria. In one small western town, the school coffee shop is the only vendor in town and attracts townspeople as well as students and staff.

In several Oregon schools, a local foundation provided the funds to set up the business with the expectation that students would learn about business practices and financial management of a small business. Many of the principals we've worked with in these schools laud the benefits of connecting students with local business people, and adding to the ambiance of the school.

While every school wouldn't want to open a coffee shop, this approach illustrates how a school can examine, and challenge, some of the "regularities" of its school day and makes changes that support the school's vision.

Structures for Extra Student Support

A major advantage of flexibility in the structure of the school day is the ability to provide support to students. When Ron works with schools on their schedule, he almost always hears about using a version of the block schedule to provide additional support to students. Structures to support students are essential to improving school learning.

There are other ways to build support for students and they involve motivating students to do well and supporting their success. Here are three examples we find useful.

Example 1: Student Rewards Program

Keith Rydell, Principal of the Vantage Career Center in Van Wert, Ohio, provided one example of a student rewards program.

> The program is called GOALS and students earn points in each category and are treated to a reward each quarter if they earn sufficient points.
>
> G = good grades
> O = good organization
> A = good attendance
> L = strong leadership
> S = strong academic skills and service

Example 2: Student Recognition Program

Beth Hill, Assistant Principal at Doss High School in Louisville, Kentucky, shares an alternate way to recognize students.

> Students can receive a "Caught being COOL" card from administrators during observations and walkthroughs. Half the card is a homework pass. The other half gets turned in for a weekly raffle.
>
> C—Conscientious
> O—On-Task
> O—Outstanding
> L—Learner

Example 3: Academic Success Time

A third option comes from Courtney Paul from Raymore-Peculiar Middle School in Missouri.

> We created *Academic Success Time* during the school day to assist students who may be struggling in a subject area. It is like tutoring during school and allows us to get to the students who might not participate in after-school tutoring.

> ### Leadership in Action
>
> A couple of years ago Ron worked with the Walled Lake Public Schools (Michigan) to identify ways that they could provide additional collaborative time for their high school teachers. He worked with a group of teachers and administrations representing all curricular areas and each of the high schools.
>
> After first identifying their goals and priorities, the group developed several prototype schedules. Following an analysis of the advantages and disadvantages of each they recommended a model that created two blocks each week for a "seminar" period. The "seminar" was designed to provide time for students to get additional instruction from teachers, to revise and resubmit assignments, and to support those students who needed additional time to complete assignments. Of course, the seminar also provided opportunity for some students to gain more in-depth knowledge in an area of interest.
>
> To find the time for two "seminar" periods, the daily schedule was modified. Formerly the high schools had a traditional seven-period day. Under the revised schedule, the day was constructed around six longer class periods (30 per week). Each class met just four times per week (28 total). The two remaining class periods were used for "seminar."

Monday	Tuesday	Wednesday	Thursday	Friday
1	7	5	4	2
2	Seminar	6	5	3
3	1	7	6	4
4	2	1	7	5
5	3	2	Seminar	6
6	4	3	1	7

Structures to Support Families

Families are essential partners in school improvement. It is important to provide them with the knowledge and tools about how they can support the school's work and their child's success.

We described some structures that support parents in Chapters 6 and 7. Chapter 6 provides a set of ideas about how to provide parents with the knowledge about your school and ways to mobilize their support for your vision. Chapter 7 discusses accountability and provided a set of strategies to engage parents in your work to improve your school.

We've found the following structures helpful to families.

Ways to Support Families

- Provide frequent communication, using multiple methods, about your school's vision and school improvement work;
- Refine your school's website to provide a place where parents can access resources about family activities that support success in school (meals, sleep, quiet time for homework, place to do homework);
- Create social media accounts to share resources and information with families;
- Organize a forum where families can share ideas about how they support student success; and
- Arrange workshops, or online training, for parents on topics that will support your vision and school improvement activities.

Structures to Support the Leader

It is also important to consider structures that will support you as a leader. Often leaders neglect their own need for support and continued learning.

We've learned that it is essential for leaders to have time to reflect on their own work, process their own learning, and consider how they can refine what they are doing to improve their school.

We encourage you to consider some of the following ideas.

Ways to Support Yourself as a Leader

- Identify a coach or mentor who you can talk with about your work. Good coaches enable leaders to process their learning and to step back and reflect on how they might improve their work.
- Stay current in the field by reading voraciously, attending conferences, and doing other professional development activities.
- Find time to meet with colleagues to share ideas and think about how you can support one another's efforts.
- Join your professional association and access its newsletters, journals, online seminars and training, and other materials.

Final Thoughts

The organization and structure of your school is one of your most powerful tools for shaping your school's program. It is critical to recognize the connection between the structure—the way you use time, arrangements for collaboration, opportunity for sustained discussion of student learning—and achieving your vision for your school.

Where Do I Begin?

If...	Then...
Your teachers want more time to work together,	Look at the section on organizing your schedule.
Your teachers discuss how challenging their students are,	Check out the section on structures for extra student support.
You want to make sure you are taking care of yourself and your leadership team,	Review the structures to support leaders chart.

9

Improving Your School
Making It Happen

Whether you are a principal, assistant principal, curriculum coordinator, or some other type of school leader, you likely have times that you feel caught between multiple roles. Although your most visible role may be as a manager, in charge of the day-to-day operations of the school or department, the more important role is your role as instructional leader and change agent.

Change as a Journey, Not an Event

We firmly believe that real instructional change begins at the classroom level. However, school-wide efforts create the climate supportive of these classroom-level changes. We've worked with principals and teachers for more than 35 years. During that time we've seen a variety of ideas discussed to improve schools. We've come to appreciate that schools are in a constant state of change. They are shaped by the demographic, social, political, and economic milieu of contemporary American society. As such they change a little each day in response to things like state or national standards, research on student learning, and parent and community demands.

As we said earlier, the most successful schools are those that recognize that change is a constant, that improvement is a journey, not an event. Change is tough. It is complex and there are often multiple paths to follow. You may even discover that you need to change direction in the middle of the journey.

Like many road trips, the journey is better when it is one shared with others. Therefore, we've found that the most successful change efforts are those defined by a shared vision and shaped by a commitment to collaboration with a school's stakeholders.

What Works and Doesn't Work With Innovation

One of the most powerful tools for sustaining change is the culture of your school. Schools characterized by a positive working relationship among teachers, active support by the principal for the change are more likely to see the project succeed. A laissez-faire attitude by the principal will virtually assure poor implementation and that the change will not succeed. Schools where the principal was active, visible, and supportive of the change experienced greater success. Principal participation bestows a stamp of legitimacy on any project and helps to sustain it after implementation.

Michael Fullan (2015) says that sustainable change boils down to three critical focal points. First, is improving relationships among staff. Second is working together to create knowledge and sharing that knowledge with one another and third is "coherence-making" or helping people make sense and give importance to their work.

Developing/Strengthening Social Relationships	<ul><li>Encourage development of social norms that support innovation and achievement for all students;</li><li>Establish teams and learning communities;</li></ul>
Learning	<ul><li>Create opportunities for people to learn in their own work setting;</li><li>Recognize that the best learning comes from peers;</li><li>Find time during the normal school day for teachers to learn from one another;</li></ul>
Cultivate Leaders at Many Levels	<ul><li>Build a cadre of leaders, formal and informal;</li><li>Provide teachers with opportunity to lead professional development and school improvement projects.</li></ul>

Source: Adapted from Fullan (2015)

Stages for Launching an Initiative

Next, in order to build a strong foundation for change, allow time to work through a series of stages. Rushing to adopt and launch an improvement plan almost always leads to implementation problems. The Oregon Small Schools Initiative (www. e3smallschools.org) identified six stages for the launch of any initiative:

1. **Study:** Time devoted to examining and learning about an issue and associated reforms. School, district, and community members can examine current practices and programs, identify gaps in student learning, and discuss how the reform can improve the educational experience of students.
2. **Stage:** During this component, a school reviews its current programs, practices, and policies and creates a shared vision for the future. Including a diverse group of people in this process helps to support, nurture, and sustain the change.
3. **Design:** This step involves the creation of standards or design frameworks that will be used to develop the specific program.
4. **Build:** During this part of the change process, the specific program components are developed and linked to the school's improvement plan.
5. **Launch:** Implementation of the plan involves mobilizing human and financial resources. It includes the provision of professional development to support the change.
6. **Sustain:** Monitoring implementation and building capacity to sustain the initiative after its launch characterizes this stage. Also included is gathering and analyzing data about the impact of the change.

We've observed schools successfully launch innovations by following these six steps. But we want to incorporate the six into a more comprehensive model for continuous school improvement, a model we call the BASE Planning Model.

The BASE Planning Model

We've been involved in many planning projects and have come to appreciate that schools are constantly changing and improving. This continuous improvement process is described many ways but we've developed our BASE model to describe a four-step process for improvement. We chose BASE because everything you do to improve your school must be built on a solid base, one that reflects research and best practice, builds support among teachers and families, and includes solid measures for success.

> **BASE Planning Model**
>
> - Begin to plan;
> - Act to implement;
> - Sustain success;
> - Evaluate and adjust.

In Chapter 1, we introduced our COMPASS model that includes seven key strategies you can use to improve your school. We like the compass as a metaphor because it shows the way and always points to "true north." Compasses are most effective when they sit on a base, one that provides a firm and steady foundation.

The four stages of the BASE model reflect a commitment to continuous improvement.

The model provides a way to organize the steps you will take to achieve your vision for school improvement. It is circular in nature and assumes that to sustain improvement you must study how you have done and that this study will naturally lead to identifying additional ways your school can continue to improve.

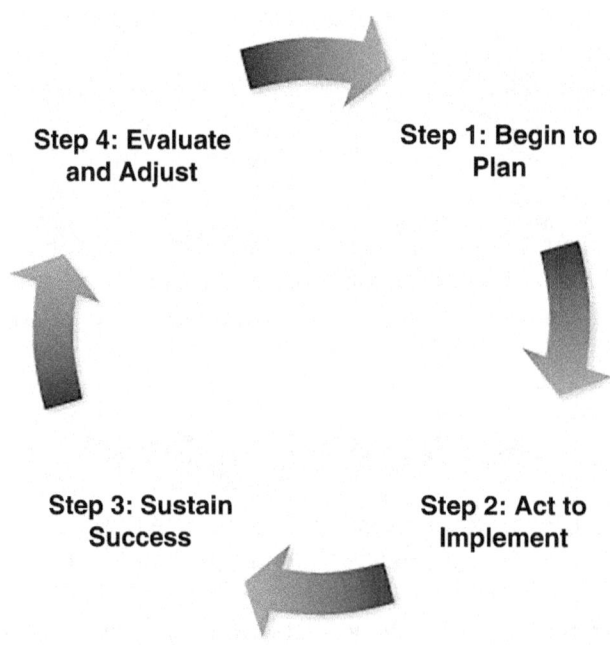

Step 1: Beginning the Planning

We've identified some strategies that you can use to work with teachers, families, and communities to improve your school. They are much like any set of tools. Not every tool works for every job. Some tasks require more than one tool. Most important is the ability to figure out which tool best fits the situation and will work most effectively.

Most importantly they recognize the importance of using an inclusive process that is focused on making your school vision a reality.

Checklist of Planning Activities

_____	1.	Are critical stakeholders involved?
_____	2.	Is there an agreed-upon mission/vision for your school?
_____	3.	Do we have the data and information about our current conditions?
_____	4.	Is there an agreed-upon process for making decisions?
_____	5.	How will we share information with others?

Use an Inclusive Process

Involving all stakeholders builds greater commitment to change. That is particularly true when you're talking about changing things that may have a long history in your school. We've learned that when teachers get actively involved in discussing ways to improve their school, they are more likely to embrace the change.

Plans for school improvement must include families and community as well as teachers and other school staff. They are integral partners in nurturing and sustaining your vision and supporting the school's efforts at home and in the greater community.

Be Clear About Group Operations

We believe strongly in a collaborative approach and have found that groups are most successful when they have a clear process to guide their deliberations.

First, we believe that use of an agreed-upon set of norms about group operations and decision-making is critical. Garmston and Wellman (1999) suggest a set of seven norms of collaboration. Information about the norms, including a self-assessment that may be used by any group is available at www.thinkingcollaborative.com.

When Ron worked at Hadley Junior High School in Glen Ellyn, Illinois, he learned about the norms they used, their "Professional Behavior Norms."

Professional Behavior Norms

1. The learning that occurs today belongs to you, and it rests largely with you.
2. Enter into the discussion enthusiastically.
3. Give freely of your experience, but don't dominate the discussion.
4. Confine your discussion to the task assigned.
5. Say what you think . . . be honest.
6. Only one person should talk at a time. Avoid private conversations while someone else is talking.
7. Listen attentively to the presentation and discussion.
8. Be patient with other participants. Appreciate their point of view.

Identify a Process for Making Decisions

It is also important to be clear about how decisions will be made. It is much easier to talk about a decision-making process at the beginning rather than when a decision must be made. Consensus is always the goal but occasionally that doesn't work and groups need to be clear about how decisions will be made.

Deciding on a course of action can be a challenge and is frequently contentious, particularly if the decision is made by voting. Voting tends to create winners and losers. There are several other ways to make decisions. They include multi-voting, use of a consensogram, or other decision-making tool.

It is important to be clear about both the task of the group and the timeline for completing their work. A teacher in one of the schools where Ron worked said, "We've found we can talk anything to death. We talk and talk and nothing gets decided or changed. Eventually the issue just goes away." Sadly, that characterizes the work in many schools. Provide a clear description of the task for the group and the date by which they should complete their work.

Provide a Common Base of Information

Everyone involved in the work should have access to the same data and have an opportunity to look at the same print and electronic resources. Often, families, students, and community members feel as though teachers and principals have "privileged" information. Occasionally even some teachers don't have the same information, especially when someone shares specific content area knowledge.

Establish a norm that no one can talk about the "research" without providing everyone access to the research. ACT, SREB, and the College Board are great sources of research. Be sure that opinions or experience are accurately labeled, not used as conclusive evidence.

One school outside of Chicago where Ron worked provided everyone involved in the discussion with a common set of readings. They included data about community demographics, information on career trends, resources on successful instructional practices, and future trends. These readings became the basis for many of the discussions about improving their school.

Anchor Your Plan in a Shared Vision

Any discussion about school improvement must be based on a shared vision. A clear and compelling vision and mission reflects the collective commitment of a school community and serves as one way to link programs and practices to a common goal.

If your school's mission statement hasn't been updated in several years, it may be time to review it and make necessary changes.

The staff at one southeastern Michigan high school recognized that their students could no longer rely on getting high-paying jobs in the automobile industry upon graduation. This change along with the general economic malaise led the principal to propose a re-examination of the school's mission. While the final statement was quite similar to the previous statement, the process led to a collective recommitment to improving the school's program focused on assuring that every graduate could meet more rigorous graduation requirements.

Vision is one of the most effective tools for personal and group motivation. Having a vision, then revisiting it regularly, helps you and your faculty focus on what is important and assists in balancing competing demands for your time and energy.

Collaboration Connection

When you are anchoring your plan in a shared vision, make sure you involved parents, students, and business partners in creating the vision, and show them how the plan links to their vision.

Commit to the Use of Data

Groups that use member's opinions as the primary source of data almost always find themselves unable to make progress. We've found that the most productive groups are comfortable gathering and analyzing data independent of individuals' experience or opinion.

It is important to anchor school improvement in data about student learning. Put together a portfolio of materials that reflects the academic expectations of students, the quality of their work, and the success on agreed-upon measures of academic success.

Another way to provide data is to ask an external observer to visit your school and provide feedback on improvement strategies.

When District 203 in Naperville, Illinois began to talk about ways to improve their middle school program, they invited Ron to visit and spend time in each of the schools. He met with several small groups of teachers, students, and parents, conducted classroom walkthroughs, and watched the general pattern of activity throughout the schools. He provided some immediate feedback to the staff at each school and, after the visit, provided a much more detailed set of recommendations to the district. These recommendations became the base for further planning.

Suggestions for Collecting Additional Data

- Conduct a self-assessment;
- Arrange for an external review by someone outside the school or district;
- Organize a shadow study of students;
- Hold a focus group discussion with students, parents, or teachers.

Step 2: Act to Implement the Plan

As complex as planning can be, implementing and sustaining those changes can be even more of a challenge. It is the implementation that forces people to face the reality that things "may be different." The reality of implementation can provoke a range of feelings including regret over abandoning familiar practices, exhilaration at the prospect of new ideas, or of being overwhelmed by the complexity of doing something new.

Checklist of Planning Activities

_____ 1. Have you created a culture of collegiality?

_____ 2. Do you have a process for gathering initial data about implementation and monitoring the implementation?

_____ 3. What opportunities have you planned for teachers to talk about and share their successes and challenges?

_____ 4. Is there an agreed-upon process for making decisions?

_____ 5. How will we share information with others?

There are several strategies and tools that you may want to consider as you work to improve your school.

Have a Plan for Monitoring the Implementation

Few changes go perfectly when implemented. Even with ample time to plan, extensive professional development, and sufficient resources, it is likely that some issues will emerge that require attention.

When this occurs, it is important to maintain a focus on improvement and not become overly defensive. We've found the following strategies to be very helpful.

Look at the Data—Gather and review any relevant data. It may be helpful to talk with groups of teachers about their experience. Look for patterns in their comments. Then use data to guide decisions. Chapter 4 provides examples of collecting data.

Provide Time to Reflect on and Discuss the Issues—Provide an opportunity for groups or individuals to share their concerns and discuss the implications. Some individuals may want to talk privately but we've found that it is helpful to have a process for structured feedback about an innovation.

There are several ways to focus this feedback but Ron has used two successfully with schools—a Plus/Delta process and the Quality Quadrant process. Both recognize that there are positive things about any implementation as well as ways to get better.

Leadership in Action

Mark Ravlin, the Executive Director for Improvement, in Adrian, Michigan, asked district planning committees to use the Plus/Delta process, a continuous improvement tool that allows a group to identify positive things about an activity as well as opportunities for improvement. Pluses identify things that are working and things that can be built upon. Deltas are things that can be improved or changed so that the plan can be more effective. They are best when action oriented and begin with a verb. Both should be reviewed and acted upon as soon as possible but action does not mean agreeing with each suggestion.

+	Δ

At Hadley Junior High in Glen Ellyn, Illinois, the planning committee used a "Quality Quadrants" tool to gather feedback from staff about suggested school improvement activities. Each teacher made comments in each of the categories and the School Improvement Team used the comments to guide their work.

Topic:	
Concerns	Kudos
Suggestions for Improvement	Questions

Don't Rush to Judgment—Be cautious about rushing to change things too quickly. It is very common for an implementation slump to occur. By that we mean that during the first few months of implementation many teachers may still be learning how to fully implement the innovation. Don't rush to change things before you have sufficient data about the need.

When Ron was working in Tempe, Arizona, one of the middle schools reorganized its instructional teams. By early October of the first year many teachers were concerned that the changes weren't working for eighth graders. After talking with students it became clear that the issue was that the eighth graders weren't committed to a new model for one year. Choosing to persevere, the staff found that there were no implementation issues the second year. The new instructional model was accepted as "just the way we do things here."

Make Appropriate Adjustments—On the other hand, you should never continue to implement a strategy that clearly is not working. If the data show that there is a need to rethink part of your plan you should do so. Often, you may learn that you need additional professional development or more time for planning. Either way, stay focused on assuring that the implementation is successful and positively benefits students.

Nurture a Collegial Culture

Schools where the leader has created a collegial culture have a better chance of success. Roland Barth, one of the nation's leading school improvement experts, suggests that:

> A precondition for doing anything to strengthen our practice and improve a school is the existence of a collegial culture in which professionals talk about practice, share their craft knowledge, and observe and root for the success of one another. Without these in place, no meaningful improvement—is possible.
>
> (Barth, 2006, p. 8)

The culture of your school is pivotal to your success. Chapter 2 discusses culture and ways you can create a culture that supports school improvement. Here are some questions you may want to consider as you begin to act on your plan.

COMPASS Tool	Leadership Strategies
Culture	• How do you create a sense of urgency about the need for improvement? • How do you nurture and support a culture of collaboration? • What do you do to develop a collegial relationship with teachers and staff?

COMPASS Tool	Leadership Strategies
Ownership and Shared Vision	• How do you engage teachers, staff, and families in developing a shared vision for your school? • What strategies do you use to build ownership and commitment to this vision? • What are the ways you've found helpful to involve stakeholders in developing a vision for an improved school?
Managing Data	• What types of data do you and your staff gather and use to guide your improvement efforts? • What are the agreed-upon measures of success for monitoring your progress? • How do you use data to measure progress?
Professional Development	• What professional development is needed to support your school's vision? • What resources are available to guide selection of professional development? • How does professional development link to the implementation of your innovation or change?
Advocacy	• What ways do you share your personal vision for your school with teachers and other staff as well as parents and the school community? • How will you and others work with parents and the larger school community to create a culture of support for your changes? • What strategy will you use to create support for the innovation among school stakeholders?
Structure	• What resources are needed to ensure success of your improvement efforts? • How do you use time, personnel, and financial resources to support your school's vision? • How will we support students, families, and the community as your school changes?
Shared Accountability	• How do you build a sense of mutual responsibility and accountability for success of the innovation? • How do we build a community commitment to our vision of an improved school?

Remove Barriers to Action

How you perceive roadblocks determines your response. Rather than seeing roadblocks as barriers, view them as opportunities. Richard Benjamin, former superintendent in Nashville and suburban Atlanta, suggested that our critics are really our best friends because they force us to be clearer about our beliefs, look more closely at our plans, and further consider the implications of our thinking.

That attitude can help a leader deal with what may appear to be insurmountable roadblocks; things that slow down or stop implementation of your innovation.

We've identified several strategies that leaders can use to find a way around the roadblocks that emerge when you're working to improve your school.

Collaboration Connection

As you identify barriers to success, consider how those barriers might be impacted by parents, students, and business partners. Determine how you might turn those barriers into benefits.

Constructively Deal With Conflict

Many school improvement plans never get implemented because either the leaders or teachers seek to avoid the conflict associated with the change. As we discussed earlier, not everyone will be supportive of change. Some will actively resist. Many will simply disengage and hope the change goes away.

There is no guarantee that implementing your plans will be free of all conflict. There are, however, some things you can do to minimize and deal constructively with conflict. You might want to try the following.

Strategies for Dealing With Conflict

- Use data and descriptions to talk about issues, not value judgments or personal interpretations;
- Focus on the present, not what was or might have been;
- Own your own ideas and feelings; use "I" as much as possible when conveying your ideas;
- Explain, do not defend;
- Be attentive to nonverbal clues and messages;
- Assume the motives of others are "honorable";
- Avoid the use of superlatives or absolutes like most, best, always, or never;
- Agree when those of another viewpoint are right;
- Use active listening skills.

We've found that one of the most useful strategies for dealing with conflict is to build positive relationships with people. When conflict arises you can draw on your reservoir of good will to help get past the difference of opinion.

Establish Accountability for Results

Accountability is critical. It should not be punitive or heavy handed, but it must be clearly defined and steadfastly implemented. Teachers and other staff must recognize their accountability for implementing any school improvement initiative, for collecting and using data to guide implementation, and for engaging in collegial conversations about their work.

As school leaders we learned that it is important to continue to support staff during implementation. Few things work exactly as planned. It is necessary to provide support and encouragement and maintain a focus on the goal.

Continue to invest in professional development. Often important implementation questions emerge only once an innovation has begun. Too often, professional development occurs prior to implementation. We've found that it is helpful to create structures that allow staff to share their experience with change and support one another during implementation.

Leadership in Action

Nancy York, principal of Fox Technical High School in San Antonio, organized a series of Café Conversations for her teachers. Each meeting was designed to focus on a single experience with increasing expectations for quality work among ninth graders. The sessions provided an opportunity for teachers to share their successes, suggest other strategies for improvement, and support trying new practices. She reported that these "teacher-to-teacher" conversations were invaluable in helping her teachers change their practices.

The conversations were held in a room that looked like an actual café. Round tables with tablecloths and a small vase of flowers contributed to the atmosphere. Snacks and beverages were available.

The café was open all day and teachers were asked to stop in during their planning time and contribute to the conversation. Chart paper was used to record ideas. By the end of the each day, this collective knowledge was available to guide further improvement.

The focus at this school was not on barriers to implementation but on identifying successes and continuing to support one another as they worked to improve the educational experience for every ninth grader.

Step 3: Sustain Success

We've found that when your work is guided by a shared vision and where teachers and other school staff are actively involved in planning and implementation that change is more likely to be sustained. When change is the result of the personal vision of one or two people, the change is more likely to be abandoned as soon as its advocates leave.

It is critical, therefore, that leaders create a culture that supports innovation and builds capacity for long-term changes in their school's program.

The third step of our planning model focuses on sustaining success. Earlier we discussed ways to monitor the implementation. We suggest you continue those activities. In addition, we encourage you to provide continued support for the implementation and begin to build internal capacity with teacher leaders so that the commitment to your improvement plan is nurtured and sustained.

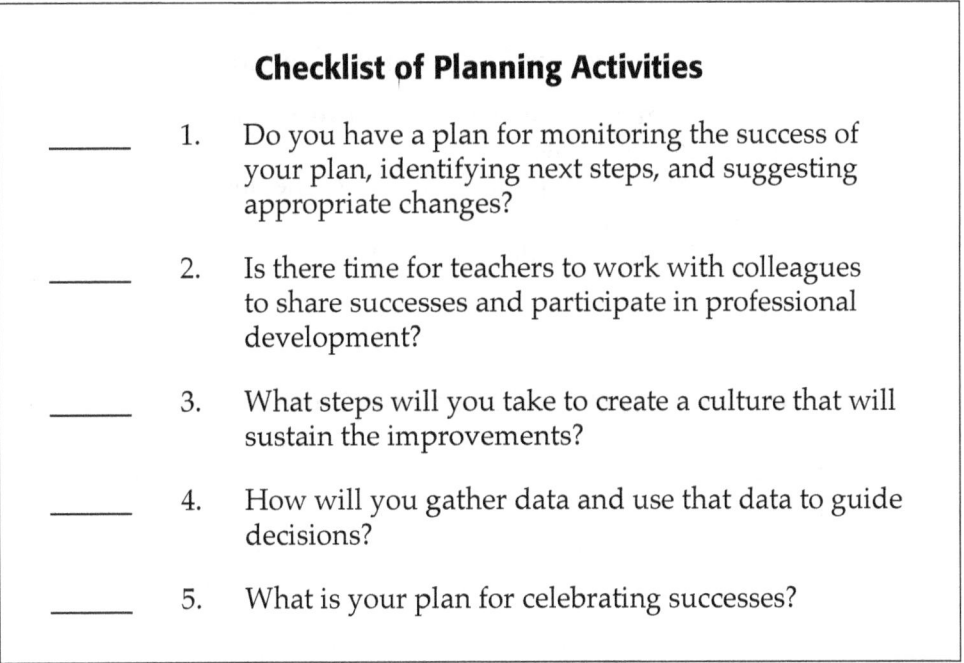

Checklist of Planning Activities

_____ 1. Do you have a plan for monitoring the success of your plan, identifying next steps, and suggesting appropriate changes?

_____ 2. Is there time for teachers to work with colleagues to share successes and participate in professional development?

_____ 3. What steps will you take to create a culture that will sustain the improvements?

_____ 4. How will you gather data and use that data to guide decisions?

_____ 5. What is your plan for celebrating successes?

Continue to Provide Support for Success

You need to build a structure that supports success. Too often support declines after the initial flurry of activity. Continue to provide professional development for teachers, collaborative time for teachers to work with one another, and supplies and materials needed to make the change succeed. That means organizing to monitor the implementation and make decisions about any modifications. It also means gathering and sharing information with stakeholders and providing time for collaboration and collegial conversation.

Monitor the Implementation—If you have not already done so it is important to organize a group to monitor the continued implementation of your plan. The group should represent all of the important groups in your school, develop the skills for collaborative work, and be committed to using data to guide decisions about further program implementation.

Identify Time for Collaboration—It is important that teachers have time to talk with colleagues about their professional work. We've found that this collaborative time is one of the catalysts for nurturing and sustaining change.

Teachers value the opportunity to meet with grade or content peers to discuss successes, diagnose ways to improve, and develop a repertoire of strategies that they can use in their own classrooms.

Here some of the ways we've found to provide collaborative time. These and other ideas were discussed in Chapter 8.

Ways to Provide Collaborative Time

- Common content or grade-level planning;
- Parallel scheduling;
- Adjusting the start and end of the day;
- Use of faculty meetings;
- Professional development days.

Create a Culture of Continuous Improvement

Can real change occur in your school or classroom if the climate and culture doesn't change? No! Real change that will be sustained over time requires a significant change in the culture of your school (see Chapter 2), in people's attitudes (see Chapter 7), and in structures and practices (see Chapter 8).

The most successful schools are places where there is a collective commitment to continuous improvement. Teachers and administrators recognize the need to regularly monitor what they are doing and make adjustments to assure the success of every student.

Regularly recognizing and celebrating positive examples of improvement will reinforce the commitment to the change. Creating structures to monitor the implementation of your plans and make appropriate adjustments signals your comfort with change. Most of all, teachers, parents, and students look to the leader for assurance that your plans are thoughtful, carefully implemented, and routinely monitored.

Use Data to Study the Results

There is often a tendency to make decisions about programs based on informal data such as people's feelings or personal experiences. While interesting, we've found that it is more useful to agree upon indicators that will be used to monitor your success.

Once you have agreed on measures of success for your improvement plan, you must routinely gather the data and use it to guide decisions that sustain implementation.

Data Considerations

_____ What are our agreed-upon measures?

_____ Have we collected the data?

_____ Is the data available for review?

_____ How will we analyze the data and use it to guide our continued planning?

_____ What additional data do we need?

Data is most useful when it includes multiple measures—different types of data and when it is longitudinal—and covers more than a single year.

Even more important than gathering data is to use it to help inform decisions. Work with others to identify patterns or trends. For example, look for trends in student test scores or patterns across students and family responses.

It is always helpful to have more than a single person look at the data. A more thoughtful analysis of data occurs when multiple perspectives and points of view are present in the discussion.

One school Ron worked with in Texas had an informal set of norms for using data.

Informal Norms

- Always use more than one type of data when making decisions;
- Support every suggestion with data, not opinions;
- Look for patterns across data sources;
- Rely most on data from more than one year.

Identify Successes and Celebrate

Effective schools celebrate small wins frequently. Have you ever heard the statement, "success breeds success?" It's true. Celebrating small gains on a regular basis can motivate teachers and students. Over time, small, steady gains add up to real growth.

Create a culture that celebrates authentic success. Keep data on school and classroom efforts, monitor their impact, and celebrate on a regular basis.

Ideas for Celebrating Success

- Recognize students who make exceptional growth in their achievement.
- Create a reward system that acknowledges efforts to improve your school and implement your changes.
- Plan a year-end school-wide celebration to reward students and teachers who promote the school's shared vision.
- Give Student of the Month Awards to students at a special luncheon with tablecloths, china, silverware, and a special menu.
- Talk with individual students about their academic success.
- Write a brief note to a teacher about something you observed.
- Create a PowerPoint presentation about your school's success to be shared with parents and community groups.
- Tell stories about students who overcame obstacles and succeeded in your school.

Other Ways to Sustain Success

First, help everyone involved see the value of your efforts to improve your school by providing clear, compelling rationale. Use data that are clear, meaningful, and linked to student success. Indicate how people can get involved in efforts to sustain the project.

Second, develop a mechanism for gathering and sharing information with teachers and other stakeholders. For example, develop a plan for talking with teachers about how they are succeeding in implementing the innovation. Ask parents about the experience of their children as your school changes its practice.

Step 4: Evaluate and Adjust

The very best schools constantly monitor their performance and identify ways to continue to make improvements. The final stage of our BASE planning model is to "Evaluate and Adjust." As we said, the planning process is circular. The decisions you make during this stage will naturally lead you to continue planning to become even better.

As with the other steps there are several important considerations. Because we discussed them earlier we will not repeat them, but here are some of the most important activities for evaluating and adjusting your plan.

Checklist of Planning Activities

1. Do you have a process to evaluate the success of your plan and identify next steps?
2. Have you gathered the data to make informed decisions about your progress?
3. What plans are developed for sharing your plans with teachers, families, and community?

Ensure Positive Dynamics Among School Personnel

It is important that you nurture and sustain a collaborative culture, one that embraces open, honest conversation about school improvement. You may discover some part of the plan needs additional attention or that additional professional development will be helpful.

That's normal. You need to resist the tendency to point fingers, to blame other people, or factors outside of your school. We don't ever believe that is helpful. The power to monitor implementation and adjust plans lies within the school with teachers and administrators.

We've worked with hundreds of schools in every region of the United States and identified behaviors that can be harmful to your success. Similarly, we've identified behaviors that can support your culture of collaboration and your work to improve your school.

Inhibitors	Facilitators
People are reluctant to share data about things that aren't working.	People are comfortable sharing data about what doesn't work. They are not penalized for doing so.
People use opinions, rather than data, to support their positions.	People support their suggestions with data, facts, and solid logic.

Inhibitors	Facilitators
People agree to a decision, yet do little to support its success.	People support mutually agreed-upon decisions and work to make the decision succeed.
People seek personal credit for success.	People credit others for success.
People disagree to improve their own interests rather than to find the best answer.	People are comfortable disagreeing and focused on finding the best response to the current issue.
People find blame, seeking culprits, rather than identifying causes.	People analyze experiences to identify ways to improve.
People blame people or conditions outside of the school for lack of success.	People accept full responsibility for successes as well as failures.
The leader avoids critical input and does not ask questions to clarify thinking.	The leader asks lots of questions, challenges thinking, and values discussion and critical insight into issues.

Source: Adapted from Collins (2009)

Data, Data, Data

Data is really important. Chapter 4 provided a more thorough discussion about how to use data to guide your decisions. But we want to be clear that decisions about monitoring, evaluating, and adjusting school improvement must use data about student learning, preferably types of data that were identified when you began planning to improve your school.

Be clear about norms you will use to talk about the data. Avoid reliance on personal opinion or "experience." But be comfortable challenging the data, asking probing questions, and identifying additional data that you may want to collect. Your initial data sources may not provide a complete picture or may have gaps.

Share What You Are Doing

It is important to have a plan for sharing your work with teachers, families, and community. Chapter 6 shared several specific strategies that you might use to share information and advocate for your school's vision.

A collective commitment to an improved school is anchored in a shared vision and confidence that the plan is collaboratively developed. Your evaluation plans should strengthen this confidence through wide dissemination of both the plan and the findings.

Sharing Results

- Share the results with stakeholder groups;
- Acknowledge both strengths and weaknesses;
- Disseminate information widely;
- Provide time for ample discussion of the results;
- Use data to guide continued planning.

Leadership in Action

When Hadley Junior High in Glen Ellyn, Illinois began a project to change the curriculum and instructional practices, the planning team developed a plan for routinely communicating with teachers and other staff and with parents.

At the end of every planning meeting a set of "talking points" were agreed to by those present. They were then shared with every teacher via e-mail. The talking points and information about every planning meeting were posted in a visible location in the main school hallway.

Months before the school began to implement the changes they held monthly "open forums" where teachers and staff could meet with members of the planning team to learn about the project and to ask questions about implementation. The meetings alternated between before school and after school.

The planning team also held a series of "Community Forums" for parents and other community members. Each forum provided an opportunity to learn about some aspect of the program changes. They also included an opportunity for parents to ask specific, targeted questions about the rationale and impact of the changes.

Final Thoughts

Because schools are under increasing pressure to improve the educational experience of students, there is a tendency to want immediate results from any innovation. This leads many schools to weave from one improvement strategy to another without clear vision and purpose, and without a clear sense of when they will be successful.

Thoughtful planning and careful implementation are important. But no step is more important than taking the time to nurture and support your improvement efforts. It is essential to monitor the implementation, gather and use data about your success, and find ways to support the teachers and other staff who work daily with your students.

Where Do I Begin?

If...	Then...
You need the most important concepts about facilitating change,	Review Michael Fullan's three critical focal points.
You want a structure that can help you lead change,	Check out the steps in the BASE model.
Meetings aren't as effective as you would like, partly due to the level and types of participation,	Look at the professional behavior norms.

10

Common Concerns

Even with the best planning and supportive implementation you will experience challenges to improving your school. The first nine chapters introduced the COMPASS model for school improvement along with a model for implementing and sustaining changes in your school.

When we work with principals and other school leaders we're often asked about how to nurture and sustain improvements. We've identified some challenges that emerge most often. This chapter will address five of the major issues we hear about when supporting school improvement efforts.

Common Concerns

How do I motivate my teachers?
How can I recruit the teachers I need to help improve our school?
How should I respond to an overly negative teacher?
How can we deal with limited resources?
How do I balance work with the rest of my life?

How Do I Motivate My Teachers?

What is the difference between a motivated and unmotivated teacher? See if the following characteristics reflect your teachers.

Characteristics

Teacher With High Motivation	Teacher With Low Motivation
Shows interest	Lack of interest
Always striving to do more	Does the minimum
Engaged	Disengaged
Focused	Distracted
Connected to leaders and other teachers	Disconnected from leaders and other teachers
Makes connections to other professional development and his/her classroom	Doesn't see relationships among aspects of professional development and his/her classroom
Secure and confident in own abilities	Concerned about self-needs
Puts forth effort	No effort

Does that look familiar? Of course, the real issue is not identifying a teacher's motivation—it's understanding and dealing with it to assure support for your ongoing improvement efforts.

Types of Motivation

There are two main types of motivation: extrinsic and intrinsic. Extrinsic motivation includes all the outside ways we try to influence a teacher, such as rewards, teacher evaluations, and student test scores. Intrinsic motivation comes from within the teacher. With extrinsic rewards, you often get temporary, short-term results. For long-term impact, it's necessary to help teachers activate their intrinsic motivation.

Intrinsic Motivation

Intrinsic motivation is that which comes from within. It is internal as opposed to external. With intrinsic motivation, teachers appreciate teaching and learning for its own sake. They enjoy learning and the feelings of accomplishment that accompany teaching, especially the success they see students experience every day. There are many benefits to intrinsic motivation. Intrinsically motivated teachers tend to prefer challenging work, are more confident about their abilities, and believe they can truly make a difference in terms of student learning.

The Foundational Elements of Intrinsic Motivation

Intrinsic motivation has two foundational elements: people are more motivated when they value what they are doing and when they believe they have a chance for success. Teachers see value in a variety of ways, but the main three are relevance, activities, and relationships.

Value

Teachers typically see value through the relevance of what you are asking them to do. That's why it's important to show practical applications for new learning. When you implement a new initiative, or ask teachers to try a new strategy in their classroom, they want to see the function. In fact, most teachers have a streaming music station playing in their heads, WII-FM—what's in it for me? That's why they ask you, "Why do we need to do this?"

When Barbara works with teachers, she knows they come into her sessions with one burning question: "How can I use this information immediately?" Adult learners are juggling so many demands, they prioritize activities and their attention based on how well something meets their immediate needs. Often we neglect to show teachers why they need to know what we are doing. Teachers are more engaged in learning when they see a useful connection to themselves.

Next, there is value in the type of learning activity you are doing. Teachers are generally more motivated by doing something than by simple "sit and get." They are also more motivated when they have ownership in the activity. Rather than simply planning a new initiative, involve teachers in the decision-making process.

Finally, teachers find value in their relationships, with you and their peers. The old adage, "they don't care what you know until they know how much you care" is true. Teachers need to feel liked, cared for, and respected by their leaders. Most teachers also need the same from their peers. If they feel isolated from other teachers and from you, they are disengaged and less likely to see value in what they are doing.

Success

Teachers are also motivated when they believe they will be successful with the new practice. And that belief is built on two building blocks.

First, the degree of alignment between the difficulty of an activity and a teacher's skill level is a major factor in self-motivation. Imagine that you enjoy playing tennis, and you have the chance to compete in a local match. You learn your opponent will be Venus Williams. How do you feel? In that situation, there's plenty of opportunity for challenge, probably too much challenge! This is where professional development is crucial. As you motivate teachers to implement a new initiative or improve their teaching, remember to also provide the appropriate support to improve their skill level.

A teacher's experiences are also an important factor. One is more likely to believe they can be successful implementing a new grouping strategy if they've already had success using small groups in their classroom. On the other hand, if a teacher continually struggles with behavioral issues during group work, they are less likely to try the new strategy.

Ways to Build Teachers' Feelings of Success

Find another teacher or mentor to assist when a teacher tries something new.
Provide time for teachers to collaborate with each other to craft high-quality lessons.
Ask a teacher to share an effective practice with colleagues.
Share stories about successful instruction in your school.

Shared Motivation

A final concept to consider is that of sharing motivation among all stakeholders. Intrinsic motivation is fostered in an overall environment of encouragement. Just as teachers share what students are doing well, it's important for parents to recognize and share the positive experiences they and their sons and daughters have with teachers. Ask your administrative assistants, custodians, and cafeteria workers to notice the "good" that is happening and to comment on it. Of course, you also want to extend the same type of actions toward them.

One specific action we saw in a school included positive notes. The school's mascot was a tiger, and they used "Paws for Praise" with their students. The principal expanded this to use with teachers. She completed the certificates whenever she saw a teacher making a difference, and then she put a basket of the certificates with pens beside the teachers' mailboxes. Teachers were encouraged to write notes to each other.

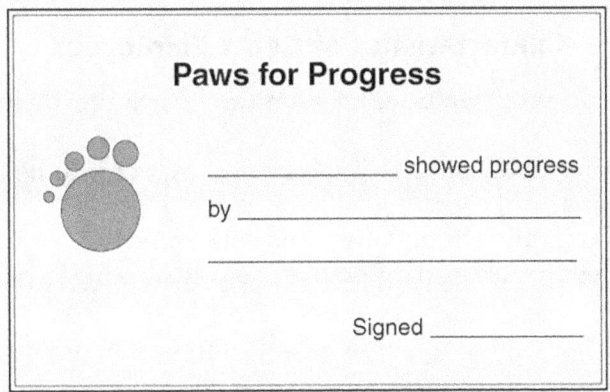

Barbara remembers visiting the school soon after this started. One teacher described the experience to her:

> I cried when I received my first note. In 20 years of teaching, I've never had another teacher tell me something specifically that I was doing well. It was so confirming and encouraging, especially since our test scores aren't as high as we'd like them to me. It reminded me that, although I'd like the scores to be better, I also need to assess myself on other things.

How Do I Recruit the Teachers I Need to Help Improve Our School?

Hiring, and then retaining the right personnel is one of the most important parts of a principal's job. When you have quality staff, your job as a leader is easier. When you have staff members who are uncooperative or ineffective, working with them can drain your time and energy. We're going to look at two aspects of working with personnel: finding the right people, and then keeping them on the staff.

A New Generation of Teachers

Baby Boomer teachers, who dominated American society for a generation, are rapidly retiring and being replaced by members of a new generation, referred to as Generation Y, one that holds very different beliefs about work, the workplace, and the way principals work with them (Coggins, 2008).

Characteristics of Gen Y Employees

- Highly educated, value education, and attribute their success to education;
- Very comfortable using technology and expect it to be available in the workplace;
- Tend to be creative, innovative, and self-confident;
- Committed to making a difference and contributing to positive social change;
- Want to be connected, updated, included, and involved in their work;
- Desire relationships with co-workers and supervisors;
- Looking for opportunities for growth, challenging work and assignments, and flexibility in work schedules;
- Possess collaborative skills, are committed to team-building, and are not afraid of accountability.

There are several strategies that leaders can use to work well with this new generation of teachers.

- Establish shared vision and goals—They want to be involved and participate in setting a vision and identifying specific, measurable goals.
- Provide leadership opportunities—They expect to be involved and to assume responsibility. They will not simply defer to more senior teachers.
- Create a positive, supportive school culture—Celebrate generational diversity and use cross-generational teams to work on curricular and instructional issues.
- Provide sound instructional leadership—They expect in-depth feedback because they want to contribute to the success of your school and expect to receive honest, open, and personalized support from you.
- Embrace technology—This generation is comfortable using technology and will expect to use all forms of technology to improve their work.
- Use data effectively and often—This generation of teacher is comfortable with accountability and the use of data. They appreciate access to user-friendly data that can be used to improve their work.

Source: Behrstock & Clifford (2009) and Rebore & Walmsley (2010)

Finding the Right People

A few years ago we met with a new principal who was hired to turn around a struggling school. At the end of his first year, 27% of his teachers left, either through retirement or resignation. Even in the best schools turnover among staff is growing as teachers become disillusioned with working conditions like low salaries and meager retirement benefits. And in a booming economy with low unemployment, skilled teachers have lots of options in other fields.

Hiring staff is often guided by district policies. The first thing you want to do is to check with the human resources department about any procedures you must follow. This often includes developing a job description and list of duties.

As you hire, it's important to standardize the hiring process. Following a standard process ensures that you will treat everyone who applies in a uniform manner. Your district may have some of these procedures in place. If not, you will need to create them for your school.

First, develop your selection criteria. Each criterion should be relevant to the work to be performed and should be free of bias so that everyone is treated the same throughout the process. If you need someone who is bilingual, include that on your list. However, as you plan, differentiate between those skills or characteristics that are required and those that are simply desirable. All criteria must be relevant to the work, but you are likely to have some nonnegotiable items and some that you would like to have in a candidate.

Next, create and use a protocol for interviews. The questions should be linked to your selection criteria, and they should be open-ended so as to provide in-depth information about the candidate. We've learned from principals that the questions you ask can tell a candidate something about your school, your priorities, and your values. Think about the questions you might ask that would align with the things valued by the new generation of teachers. You might consider questions such as, "What do you see as your strengths related to this position?" "What leadership skills do you bring that could be immediately used to improve our school?" "Imagine you were offered the position and accepted it, and it is one year later. What was the best part of your first year, and what was your biggest challenge?" After you draft your questions, always assess them to be sure you avoid any questions that might be unlawful.

Finally, follow your process. In some cases, you may realize early in the interview that a person is not the best fit for the job. However, respect the candidate and the process and finish the interview. After you hire someone, be sure to send a follow-up note or e-mail to all candidates, notifying them that they did not get the job and thanking them for their interest in the position. A little courtesy goes a long way at this point. Many teacher candidates are looking at positions in multiple districts and you might end up with someone other than your first choice.

Keeping the Right People

Whether you have hired your own staff or inherited them from a former administrator, you want to keep the right people. Schools are basically people places, so it is important to nurture and cultivate talented employees and make them feel valued and part of the organization.

Steps to Create a "People-Oriented" Workplace

- See each person as an individual, as unique.
- Provide opportunities for each individual to assume responsibility.
- Remind individuals about the need for strict compliance with rules but consider exceptions when appropriate.
- Create a place where people seek to learn from the experience and consider other alternatives rather than lay blame when things don't work out.
- Value listening and respecting varied points of view.
- Allow flexibility for people to teach or organize their classrooms in different ways.
- Provide opportunities for leadership to everyone.

As a leader, you have three keys that have been shown to improve employee satisfaction: effective communication, engagement in significant tasks, and valuing and respecting different points of view.

Effective Communication

Your first key to employee satisfaction is your ability to communicate effectively with your employees. When communicating, focus more energy on listening than speaking. Remember that much communication occurs through body language, so be attentive to nonverbal cues about meaning. Be aware of any power relationship (supervisor-supervisee, evaluator-evaluatee) that may be influencing the situation. Throughout the conversation, ask clarifying questions and probe for deeper meaning in response to any comments. Overall, focus on mutual problem solving and look for win-win solutions. And always identify next steps for each person, which will clarify each person's responsibilities.

Engagement in Significant Tasks

Next, quality employees are more likely to be satisfied if they are engaged in significant tasks. Identify meaningful ways to involve employees in school decision-making rather than involving them in trivial decisions, such as the location of a copier. For all tasks, be clear in defining the task, the desired or required timeline, and any resources that will be provided. Earlier in the chapter we discussed the new generation of teachers and the characteristics they look for in the workplace.

Valuing and Respecting Different Points of View

Another key to retaining employees is your choice to respect points of view that differ from your own. Make it clear that you value freedom of expression, and reinforce that in every aspect of your job. When hearing unpleasant news, rather than reacting defensively, be open and probe for understanding by asking clarifying questions. Structure meetings and other activities to model openness, and use a decision-making process that requires exploration of alternatives and an analysis of advantages and disadvantages. Activities such as these will reinforce for your employees that you are open to differing perspectives.

How Should I Respond to an Overly Negative Teacher?

One of the biggest challenges you will face is the resistance that emerges from teachers. It may manifest itself through the voice of a single, highly vocal, resistant teacher, or more subtly through the chatter from a small group of teachers or other staff.

Addressing the Resistance

Not everyone who resists change does so because of ulterior motives. Often there is a conflict between their personal beliefs and values and the proposed changes. In Michigan many educators and parents opposed the idea of increasing the mathematics requirement for high school graduation. A survey found that many of those resisting the idea were concerned that the new requirement would increase dropouts. Their motives were anchored in concern for students, not outright resistance to an idea. As the new requirements were implemented, much of the resistance faded when students were provided additional academic support, multiple opportunities to succeed, and different instructional approaches.

While some people resist, just to resist, most don't. They are genuinely concerned about the proposed change. They either don't see the value in the change or they have concerns about how successful the change will be.

Leaders need to recognize the diverse feelings and concerns when you begin to work on any improvement plan. Individuals progress through the stages in a developmental manner. Not everyone will move at the same pace or have the same intensity of feeling.

Personal concerns about knowledge of the plans often characterize the first stage. As you begin to launch your plans, management concerns emerge. Once you're under way teachers become more interested in the effects of the change on students and on their classrooms.

Handling the Toxic Teacher

But occasionally, there is one individual who resists in a way that can disrupt the entire school, and detract from the work of other teachers and staff. They're often toxic because in addition to causing disgruntlement in the workplace, they also spread their disgruntlement to others.

What a Leader Can Do

Here are six steps experts recommend for managing the toxic employee (Gallo, 2016).

- **Dig Deeper**—Always take a close look at the behavior and what might be causing it. It may be because of factors outside of school, or unhappiness with colleagues or opportunities for advancement. This information may be used to coach the teacher or suggest resources such as the employee assistance program.
- **Provide Direct Feedback**—Toxic employees may be oblivious to their behavior and its effect on the school and other employees. Porath (2016) suggests that they may be too focused on their own needs and it may be necessary to let them know how annoying they are. Be explicit and cite examples. Just don't dwell on it and allow them to control the conversation. In addition, Porath found that 4% of people engage in this kind of behavior because they think they can get away with it and they think it is just fun.

- **Explain Consequences**—Let the teacher know about the costs of their continued behavior. It may mean limited opportunity for professional development or travel to conferences or even transfer or dismissal. In some states non-tenured teachers can be dismissed without providing a reason.
- **Understand That Some People Don't Change**—It's always good to be optimistic and to support and encourage employees. But that doesn't work with everyone. If that's the case you may need to talk with your human resources office about next steps.
- **Document Everything**—As with all personnel issues, be sure and document all of your conversations, your meetings, and suggestions for improvement. This helps to establish a pattern of behavior.
- **Isolate the Toxic Person and "Immunize" the Team**—If the toxic behavior persists and the person remains in your school, you can isolate them and minimize their impact. Don't assign them a role in your planning. Don't include them in any groups planning implementation or professional development. If you organize work groups, minimize their role if any. You can rearrange rooms, schedule fewer meetings, and lessen the contact with colleagues. If other employees come to you about their toxic colleague, hold one-on-one conversations but be discreet and coach them on how to minimize contact and interaction.
- **Don't Get Distracted**—Finally, a toxic teacher has a way of consuming your time and energy. Don't allow that to happen. Find time to counteract their behavior by working and interacting with employees who are supportive and engaged. And, of course, take care of your own work-life balance, something discussed later in this chapter.

Focus on Students

It seems so obvious to always think about students first. But we've found that when complex and difficult issues arise, student interests are often secondary to the interests of teachers, parents, or community. Part of the problem is that everything that people want to do is always described as being "in the best interests of students." Often diametrically opposed ideas are both described that way.

William Roberts, Principal of Los Altos High School in Hacienda Heights, California led significant changes in his school's program. He said that he always asked his staff, "How would you want your child to be treated? What would you want their program to be like?" He found that for many of his teachers those questions forced them to consider the needs of their students through their perspective as a parent. It changed the conversation.

How Can We Deal With Limited Resources?

No school is immune from the need to plan for a future with declining, or at the best, stable resources. Schools are caught between expectations for improved student performance and the reality that there are fewer human and financial resources to support the program. Almost universally the issue is one of how to be both efficient and more effective. Secretary of Education Arne Duncan (2010) calls the current situation "the New Normal," meaning that schools will see increasing demands for performance in a climate of declining resources.

There are generally three responses. First, you can identify areas where you might reduce expenses by eliminating programs or reducing budgets. But in many schools these efficiencies have already been achieved. Second, you can consider alternative ways of doing things you're already doing. For example, some rural schools have shifted to a four-day week to reduce costs of transportation, food service, and office support. Some have begun to work together by combining programs, sharing teachers, or sharing central office resources. In Michigan one district contracted with a nearby district for a portion of the superintendent's time. Others consolidated human resources or business services. Third, you can prioritize what you are doing. This is often difficult, even when you use data, because it is often seen as valuing one program more than others. If you prioritize, be sure to anchor your decisions in your school's vision and mission.

The Four "R's"

Some schools have learned that reducing every program a little isn't very effective. Schools cannot simply cut their way out of this crisis. It may be necessary to focus on fewer things and do them really well. Always be sure someone is advocating for the neediest students, those requiring the most support. These challenging decisions are almost always better when teachers, families, and other stakeholders are included.

Everything must be on the table—the way we use technology, time, space, instructional materials, and personnel. Protecting learning opportunities for children must be the highest priority, but teachers and administrators must attend to their own personal wellbeing while making these very difficult decisions as well. Especially important is that the voices of those children and families most in need be heard in all of the decision-making processes as well.

The strategies fall into four categories, the "Four R's"—reduce, refine, reprioritize, and regenerate (Johnston & Williamson, 2014). Many of these approaches are not easy, and may not be enthusiastically embraced by staff, parents, students, or even community. They are most successful when decisions are made in a collaborative and inclusive environment, one that welcomes open debate and values consensus building.

The Four "R's"

> Reduce;
> Refine;
> Reprioritize;
> Regenerate.

Reduce

Reductions are often the most common response to declining resources. Cuts should be made in a fair, reasonable, transparent, and humane manner. Reducing the budget most often involves freezing current spending, making across-the-board cuts, identifying targeted reductions, or eliminating programs.

Reducing budgets is something no one likes, but almost everyone understands. What people want is information about the impact it will have on them, their programs, or their children.

We believe good fiscal decision-making has several elements.

Elements of Good Fiscal Decision-Making

> **High-Quality Information**—Help people understand deficits, steps taken to soften the effect and the data used to make decisions.
> **Consistency of Message**—People rely on those they trust (including social media friends) for information and not necessarily school leaders. Invest in "internal public relations" to make sure everyone in the school is giving the same message about reductions.
> **Confidentiality**—Be careful what you say and to whom you say it. If reductions target a program or specific personnel, don't let a leak reveal the information first.
> **Trust in the Organization**—When school staff support a shared vision of the school's mission, they are more likely to deliver a consistent message.
> **Address Key Issues Directly**—Deal with real concerns as soon as possible. Everyone wants to know if they will lose their job. Make sure messages are accurate and lesson anxiety.
> **Don't Make Promises**—Statements made early can feel like a commitment and trust will be damaged if your "promise" can't be kept.

> **Dissent**—Recognize that dissenting opinions are always uncomfortable but are important. They can reveal problems that weren't thought about and they can give you clues about the resistance you will encounter.
> **Different Audiences**—Consistency of your message is critical but different audiences want different information. Teachers will be concerned about jobs. Parents may be concerned about programs for their children or school safety. The community may be concerned with the image of the school or community.
> **Someone Will Be Unhappy**—Budget cuts are always tough and someone will always be upset and angry about the outcome.
>
> *Source:* From Johnston and Williamson (2014)

Refine

Schools can also reorganize, streamline, or improve efficiency without cutting core programs. The focus is finding the most efficient way to achieve goals rather than making a fundamental change.

The Annenberg Institute for School Reform (Barnes, 2004) suggests four areas where refinements work.

Four Areas to Refine

> Human Resource Use and Development;
> School Organization;
> Fiscal and Technical Resources;
> Social Resources.

Human Resource Use and Development

There are several general strategies that you can consider to refine the human resource mix in your school (Petrilli, 2012).

- Ask teachers to take on additional responsibilities for additional pay.
- Reduce ancillary positions or specialized personnel.
- Trade down by getting services for lower cost. For example, use county health personnel rather than school nurses.
- Invest in staff by cross-training so teachers can teach in more than one area.

School Organization

Take a look at how your school is organized and the structures that are part of the year. Modest increases in class size, while not desired, are a refinement, as is redesigning the school schedule.

Fiscal and Technical Resources

First, spend money on things that work and stop spending money on things that don't. That may require a tough examination of past practices and a willingness to abandon things that have been in place for a long time.

Thoughtfully integrate technology in ways that will strengthen and enhance the program. Most states permit online courses and they are a good option for expanding and enriching the curriculum. Some schools teach foreign language by using Rosetta Stone or some other online software system rather than a traditional classroom. Or, arrange online tutoring from low-cost college students, retirees, or volunteers rather than more costly full-time employees.

Social Resources

Community assets are a tremendous resource. Partnerships are ways of using community assets to increase your resources. Think about potential partners in your community and devote time to cultivating relationships.

Reprioritize School Goals

This is perhaps the most complex of the four strategies because of the need to think deeply about the school's mission and values, and which activities are most closely aligned with the mission. Rather than tinkering with programs, reprioritizing reconsiders maintaining programs that don't align with the school's mission.

There is no single process that makes reprioritizing easy. Your school is composed of multiple interest groups who will want to be involved. The most contentious decisions in any organization are around scarce resources and how they are used (Bolman & Deal, 2017).

Rethinking some of a school's fundamental operations can lead to new priorities. In many districts that has included thinking about a four-day week, reducing transportation for middle and high school students, changing the schedule, using technology more including online courses and online professional development, and securing other funding from local, state, or federal grants to pay for some programs or services.

When reprioritizing it is important to use a process that is inclusive of all interest groups, that is focused on building consensus, and that values disparate points of view.

Regenerate

Generating additional resources or finding new sources of funds to support innovation and growth is another strategy. Additional funding can come from business or community partnerships, school foundations, grants, fees, and entrepreneurial activity.

Business Partnerships

Business partnerships are typically established between a school, or district, and a local business or a national partner with a local presence (Johnston & Williamson, 2014). They are most successful when there is a mutually supportive relationship and the partners commit themselves to specific goals and activities benefiting students.

While additional resources are good for a school, they are also good for a business that may have enhanced good will and a stronger presence in the community (Council for Corporate and School Partnerships, n.d.).

Barbara worked with one school district that was facing a challenge with struggling readers. They found that if poor readers could listen to a text prior to experiencing it in class, they performed better. However, many of the text materials were not available in audio format. The district asked local businesses to support their initiative in one of two ways: to purchase audio equipment students could use at home and for their employees to read and record the text. Businesses were happy to participate, and it allowed employees to support the schools without taking time off work.

Community Partnerships

Community partnerships bring together the resources of local businesses, service clubs, nonprofit agencies, volunteers, churches, colleges, and universities, almost anyone with an interest in children and young people. They are a powerful social resource that schools can tap into to support their educational programs (Johnston & Williamson, 2014).

School Foundations

A foundation is a legal entity that is created to provide support for a cause, in this case, your school or school district. Many schools and school districts create their own foundations to support educational programs. You will want specialized legal advice when creating a foundation and many schools we've worked with use a local attorney who donates their services.

Grants

Many schools have become much more aggressive in seeking grants and contracts. A consortium of five small districts Ron worked with in Oregon sought a state grant to pay for adding interactive television so that they could share Spanish, accelerated math, and chemistry teachers. The teachers would rotate among the five high schools but be able to interact with students on all five campuses.

This same consortium shared the costs of a grant writer and by the end of the first year found that the position was more than paid for by the number of grants that were secured.

Resources for Grant Funding

Grants Alert—http://grantsalert.com;
US Department of Education—www.rants.gov;
NEA Foundation—Other grants and fellowships; www.neafoundation.org.

How Do I Balance Work With the Rest of My Life?

Almost everyone recognizes the importance of work-life balance. The issue for most is how to create the balance. Unfortunately, the literature has not found a single set of strategies that works for every individual. But fortunately, the literature does provides a comprehensive set of tools and strategies that individuals can consider as they seek the balance appropriate for them.

Understand Yourself

In order to achieve work-life balance you need to think about yourself, your patterns, and your aspirations. Values and beliefs shape our actions and impact our personal set of life experiences. Here are some suggestions for understanding yourself.

- *Define what "greater balance" means for you.* What would it look like if it was achieved? Who else should be part of the conversation about work-life balance (Chakravarty, 2011)?

- *Think about what you value.* Being clear about your values is one key to establishing balance, or at least understanding why you don't have balance. A conflict in values can create stress and disrupt the balance we seek. For example, you may value getting to work early but also value spending a little time with your spouse, children, or significant other before your day begins. Perhaps you value finishing your work before you leave for the day, but also value attending your children's after-school activities or being available to help with childcare or household chores (Graham, 2002).
- *Identify your patterns.* Think about how you organize your day. What things always get accomplished and what things deferred? What choices do you make about sleep, diet, and exercise? Do you schedule breakfast meetings or do you reserve that time for transitioning from personal time to work (Graham, 2002)?
- *Understand your natural workday rhythms.* People have their own natural rhythms. Identify your rhythms and patterns during the day. Some people prefer an unstructured start to the day, others prefer to jump right into their work. Figure out your rhythms and structure your work around those natural patterns. Pay attention to your patterns over the day, assuring adequate breaks and time to rejuvenate (Chakravarty, 2011; Uscher, 2011).

Set Realistic Goals and Expectations

Finding work-life balance is about setting priorities and managing time (Graham, 2002; Uscher, 2011). Our perceptions, attitudes, and assumptions often shape the expectations we have for ourselves. Here are some suggestions for setting realistic goals.

- *Check out assumptions about your work.* Talk with your supervisor about priorities and balance. Help your supervisor understand the right balance for your life and how that balance can be achieved. We often set our unrealistic standards for our own performance. Good supervisors know the importance of work-life balance and how a lack of balance can negatively impact an individual's work and the health of the entire organization (Chakravarty, 2011; Hall & Richter, 1989).
- *Talk with your family or significant other* about priorities and schedules. Much of the stress about work-life balance is a result of tension with those we care about the most. Talking about the issues and being open to finding solutions helps lessen the stress (Graham, 2002).
- *Include time for yourself* and your own personal interests among your goals. Be sure to allow time for adequate sleep and exercise (Mayo Clinic, 2012).

Part of this process is to create a vision of where you want to be. After considering the suggestions above, create a sample vision card based on your thoughts.

Sample Vision Card

I am passionate about helping each student learn and achieve at high levels. Within three years, this school will be the highest performing school in the district, with no differences among subgroups of students. In order to achieve that goal, I will update my action plan at the start of each month in order to identify specific actionable steps. Since I am most productive in the morning, I will block time each morning to focus on my vision and plan. Each week, I will update teachers and other stakeholders on our progress and ask for help when needed. Finally, unless there is an emergency, I will leave school by 5pm in order to have time to go to the gym and be home for time with family and/or partners.

Managing Work-Life Balance

Even with realistic goals and an understanding of your own values, managing work-life balance can be a challenge. Here's advice from others about work-life balance.

- *Build time for yourself into your schedule.* When you plan your week, include time for exercise, for hobbies or activities, for family and friends. Actually add it to the schedule just like any other professional commitment. Most importantly "be proactive about scheduling" (Stack, 2010). When leaders don't take care of themselves and recognize the need for balance, it negatively impacts the whole organization (Mayo Clinic, 2012).
- *Make boundaries clear.* Negotiate, and legitimize, boundaries between work and your personal life. Be really clear about when you are available for work activities and the time you preserve for family and personal time. Take control of your day and week. There may be times during the day when your door is closed and you're working on projects, other times when you are available. The same is true for your personal and family time. Give yourself permission to delay responding to texts or e-mail (Chakravarty, 2011).
- *Identify a mentor, coach or friend with whom you can talk.* Being a leader, particularly in a small school, can be an isolated job. There's evidence that leaders need someone with whom they can talk, and

share problems, including frustrations about work-life balance. The person must be someone you trust and there is some evidence that a person outside of education, who doesn't share the same expectations, can be the best listener (Lord, Atkinson, & Mitchell, 2008).

- *Pay attention to sleep, exercise, and diet.* Busy people often neglect sleep, exercise, and may not eat regularly, or make unhealthy choices about what they eat. Be attentive to the need for adequate sleep, and build time for exercise, even a walk around the outside of the school, into your schedule. Don't grab lunch "on the run" or eat while working on other things. Instead take short mental breaks, eat a healthy snack, and drink plenty of water (Mayo Clinic, 2012; Uscher, 2011).
- *Talk with your partner.* The quality of your personal relationships impacts everyone around you. Talk openly with your partner about work-life balance, about priorities, about scheduling, and about how to support one another (Graham, 2002).
- *Stop doing some things.* Analyze your schedule and your activities. Identify things that you don't need to do, or don't need to do as frequently. Give yourself permission to drop them from your routine (Anderson, 2013; Mayo Clinic, 2012).
- *Delegate and/or divide work.* Often a leader thinks they must do everything or respond to every request. They often worry about losing control. There are often others in your school who can do some of the work. Some people enjoy the opportunity to learn a new task or perhaps they aspire to being a school leader and want some experience with leadership tasks. Become comfortable delegating tasks or subdividing the work among several people (Anderson, 2013; Mayo Clinic, 2012).

Communicate, Communicate, Communicate

While planning is helpful to work-life balance, even more helpful is communication with your supervisor and with your spouse or significant other. Helping others understand what you are doing as well as how you are managing your work without burning yourself out is critical.

Final Thoughts

Every school leader we've met is working to improve their school. It's a major commitment of time and energy to transform a school and achieve all it can be. This chapter explored five of the major concerns we hear from leaders about how to assure sustained improvement.

References

Adventure Associates. (2009). *Teamwork skills: Fist-to-five measuring support*. Retrieved online May 30, 2009, from www.adventureassoc.com/resources/newsletter/nltc-fist-to-five.html

Anderson, A. (2013). Work-life balance: 5 ways to turn it from the ultimate oxymoron into a real plan. *Forbes*. Retrieved from www.forbes.com/sites/amyanderson/2013/07/26/work-life-balance-the-ultimate-oxymoron-or-5-tips-to-help-you-achieve-better-worklife-balance/#45a858a05841

Astuto, T. A., Clark, D. L., Read, A., McGree, K., Fernandez, L., & deK, P. (1993). *Challenges to dominant assumptions controlling educational reform*. Andover, MA: Regional Laboratory for the Educational Improvement of the Northeast and Islands.

Barnes, F. (2004, April). *Inquiry and action: Making school improvement part of daily practice*. Providence, RI: Annenberg Institute for school Reform at Brown University. Retrieved from http://annenberginstitute.org/tools/guide/SIGuide_intro.pdf

Barth, R. (2006). Improving relationships within the schoolhouse. *Educational Leadership*, 63(6), 8–13.

Behrstock, E., & Clifford, M. (2009). *Leading gen Y teachers: Emerging strategies for school leaders*. Washington, DC: National Comprehensive Center for Teacher Quality.

Blackburn, B. (2000). *Barriers and facilitators to effective staff development: Perceptions from award-winning practitioners* (Unpublished doctoral dissertation), University of North Carolina at Greensboro, Greensboro.

Blackburn, B. (2012). *Rigor is not a four-letter word* (1st ed.). New York: Routledge.

Blackburn, B. (2015). *Motivating struggling learners: 10 strategies for student success*. Larchmont, NY: Routledge.

Blackburn, B. (2018). *Rigor is not a 4-letter word* (3rd ed.). New York: Routledge.

Blackburn, B. (2019). *Differentiation and rigor in the classroom*. New York: Routledge.

Blackburn, R., Blackburn, B., & Williamson, R. (2018). *Advocacy from A to Z*. New York: Routledge.

Bolman, L., & Deal, T. (2017). *Reframing organizations: Artistry, choice and leadership* (6th ed.). Hoboken, NJ: John Wiley & Sons, Inc.

Borko, H. (2004). Professional development and teacher learning: Mapping the terrain. *Educational Researcher*, 33(8), 3–15.

Bower, M. (1996). *Will to manage*. New York: McGraw-Hill.

Chakravarty, D. (2011). Working out a balance. *Money Today*. Retrieved from www.businesstoday.in/moneytoday/careers/right-balance-professional-and-personal-life/story/16457.html

Coggins, C. (2008). The post-boomer teacher crunch. *Education Week, 27*(32), 26–27.

Collins, J. (2009). *How the mighty fall*. New York: Harper Collins.

Council for Corporate and School Partnerships. (n.d.). *A how-to guide for school-business partnerships*. Concord, NH: New Hampshire Scholars. Retrieved from www.nhscholars.org/School-Business%20How_to_Guide1.pdf

David, J. (2009). Collaborative inquiry. *Educational Leadership, 66*(4), 87–88.

Deal, T., & Kennedy, A. (1982). *Corporate cultures: The rites and rituals of corporate life*. Reading, MA: Addison-Wesley.

Deal, T., & Peterson, K. (1999). *Shaping school culture*. San Francisco, CA: Jossey-Bass.

Deal, T., & Peterson, K. (1990). *The principal's role in shaping school culture*. Washington, DC: US Department of Education.

Deal, T., & Peterson, K. (2016). *Shaping school culture* (3rd ed.). San Francisco, CA: Jossey-Bass.

Dean, C., Hubbell, E., Pitler, H., & Stone, B. (2012). *Classroom instruction that works* (2nd ed.). Alexandria, VA: ASCD.

DuFour, Ri., DuFour, Re., Eaker, R., & Many, T. (2006). *Learning by doing: A handbook for professional learning communities at work*. Bloomington, IN: Solution Tree.

Duncan, A. (2010, November 17). *The new normal—doing more with less: Speech to the American enterprise institute*. Washington, DC: US Department of Education. Retrieved from www.ed.gov/news/speeches/new-normal-doing-more-with-less-secretrary-arne-duncans-remarks-american-enterprise-institute

Fletcher, A. (2002). Fist-to-five consensus-building. *Freechild project*. Retrieved July 1, 2009, from www.freechild.org/Firestarter/Fist2Five.htm

Fullan, M. (2001). *Leading in a culture of change*. San Francisco, CA: Jossey-Bass.

Fullan, M. (2015). *The new meaning of educational change* (5th ed.). New York: Teachers College Press.

Gallo, A. (2016). How to manage a toxic employee. *Harvard Business Review*. Retrieved February 15, 2019 from https://hbr.org/2016/10/how-to-manage-a-toxic-employee

Garmston, R., & von Frank, V. (2012). *Unlocking group potential to improve schools*. Thousand Oaks, CA: Corwin.

Garmston, R., & Wellman, B. (1999). *The adaptive school: A sourcebook for developing collaborative groups*. Norwood, MA: Christopher-Gordon.

Glickman, C., Gordon, S., & Ross-Gordon, J. (2018). *Supervision and instructional leadership: A developmental approach* (10th ed.). New York: Pearson.

Gold, Y., & Roth, R. (1999). *The transformational helping professional: Mentoring and supervising reconsidered*. Boston: Allyn & Bacon.

Graham, J. (2002). *Balancing work and family: Bulletin #4186 University of Maine Extension Service*. Retrieved from https://extension.umaine.edu/publications/4186e/

Hall, D., & Richter, J. (1989). Balancing work life and home life: What can organizations do to help? *The Academy of Management Executive, 2*(3), 213–223.

Henebery, B. (2017). *How to market your school effectively*. Retrieved online February 1, 2019 from www.theeducatoronline.com/au/news/how-to-market-your-school-effectively/242467

Hord, S. (2009). Professional learning communities. *Journal of Staff Development, 30*(1), 40–43.

Hoy, W., & Tarter, C. J. (2008). *Administrators solving the problems of practice: Decision-making concepts, cases, and consequences* (3rd ed.). Boston: Pearson Education.

Johnston, J. H., & Williamson, R. (1998). Listening to four communities. *NASSP Bulletin, 82*(597), 44–52.

Johnston, J. H., & Williamson, R. (2014). *Leading schools in an era of declining resources*. New York: Routledge.

Juarez, K. (2007). *Charrette protocol*. Retrieved February 19, 2019 from www.schoolreforminitiative.org/download/charrette-protocol/

Learning Forward. (2019). *Standards for professional learning*. Retrieved online January 2, 2019 from https://learningforward.org/standards

Lord, P., Atkinson, M., & Mitchell, H. (2008). *Mentoring and coaching for professionals: A study of the research evidence*. National Foundation for Educational Research. Retrieved from www.nfer.ac.uk/media/2003/mcm01.pdf

Maslow, A. H. (1968). *Toward a psychology of being*. New York: John Riley.

Mayo Clinic. (2012). *Work-life balance: Tips to reclaim control*. Retrieved from www.mayoclinic.org/healthy-lifestyle/adult-health/in-depth/work-life-balance/art-20048134?reDate=22022019

McGowen, H. (2013). *12 inexpensive and easy ways to market your school*. Retrieved online January 15, 2019, from http://sounding-board.net/12-inexpensive-and-easy-ways-to-market-your-school

National Staff Development Council. (2001). *National staff development council's standards for staff development*. Retrieved April 19, 2009, from www.nsdc.org/standards/index.cfm

Oxley, D., Barton, R., & Klump, J. (2006). Creating small learning communities. *Principal's Research Review, 1*(6), 3.

Peterson, K. D., & Deal, T. E. (2002). *The shaping school culture fieldbook*. San Francisco, CA: Jossey-Bass.

Petrilli, M. (2012). *How districts can stretch the school dollar: Policy brief*. Dayton, OH: Thomas B. Fordham Institute.

Porath, C. (2016). *Mastering civility: A manifesto for the workplace*. New York: Grand Central Publishing.

Rebore, R., & Walmsley, A. (2010). *Recruiting and retaining generation Y teachers*. Thousand Oaks, CA: Corwin Press.

Rettburg, J. (2008). *Blogging*. Cambridge: Polity Press.

Schein, E. (2016). *Organizational culture and leadership* (5th ed.). San Francisco, CA: Jossey-Bass.

Shapiro, J., & Stefkovich, J. (2016). *Ethical leadership and decision-making in education* (4th ed.). Mahwah, NJ: Lawrence Erlbaum Associates.

Stack, L. (2010). *Super competent: The six ways to perform at your productive best*. Hoboken, NJ: John Wiley & Sons.

Uscher, J. (2011). 5 tips for better work-life balance. *WebMD*. Retrieved from www.webmd.com/women/features/balance-life#1

Williamson, R. (2009). *Scheduling to improve student learning*. Westerville, OH: National Middle School Association.

Williamson, R., & Blackburn, B. (2016). *The principalship from A to Z* (2nd ed.). New York: Routledge.

Williamson, R., & Blackburn, B. (2018). *Rigor in your school: A toolkit for leaders* (2nd ed.). New York: Routledge.

Williamson, R., & Johnston, J. H. (2005). Leadership in the middle level school. In V. Anfara, G. Andrews, & S. Mertens (Eds.), *The encyclopedia of middle grades education*. Greenwich, CT: Information Age Publishing.

Williamson, R., & Johnston, J. H. (2012). *The school leader's guide to social media*. New York: Routledge.

For Product Safety Concerns and Information please contact our EU
representative GPSR@taylorandfrancis.com
Taylor & Francis Verlag GmbH, Kaufingerstraße 24, 80331 München, Germany

www.ingramcontent.com/pod-product-compliance
Lightning Source LLC
Chambersburg PA
CBHW080937300426
44115CB00017B/2857